PRAISE FOR *THE WOMAN'S ADVANTAGE*

"Reading this book is like sitting in a room with 20 remarkable women who are eager to share their experiences. Cantando shows that success is not some special gift of the few, but an achievable goal for anyone who has the passion and commitment to play the game."
LINDA TISCHLER, SENIOR WRITER, *FAST COMPANY*

"One of the best business books I've ever read! Mary conveys sophisticated business concepts in a format that is like having a conversation with a trusted friend."
SUSAN PHILLIPS BARI, FOUNDER AND PRESIDENT, WOMEN'S BUSINESS ENTERPRISE NATIONAL COUNCIL

"Any woman who owns a business or dreams of starting one, must read The Woman's Advantage. *Each of these 20 women has built a multimillion-dollar empire leveraging a woman's particular perspectives and strengths. To have all these insights and experiences collected in one place–what an incredible resource!"*
MARTI BARLETTA, AUTHOR, *MARKETING TO WOMEN*, AND FOUNDER/CEO, THE TRENDSIGHT GROUP

"Women are not on the rise. They have already risen, and have been ahead of the curve for more than a decade. This is not just a guidebook for women to succeed in business, it's also a must-read for every man trying to do business with them."
JEFFREY GITOMER, AUTHOR, *THE LITTLE RED BOOK OF SELLING*

*"*The Woman's Advantage *is full of golden nuggets of entrepreneurial information. It's a fabulous book to keep for a reference (and inspiration) as your woman-owned business grows and blossoms."*
PENNY POMPEI, PRESIDENT AND CEO, NATIONAL WOMEN'S BUSINESS CENTER

"Be bold, be brave, think big and carry a copy of The Woman's Advantage *with you at all times. This volume is more than just a book you need to own, it's the bible for women business owners. If you use it as your reference guide throughout the lifecycle of your business, you will indeed have the advantage."*
AMY MILLMAN, PRESIDENT, SPRINGBOARD ENTERPRISES

THE WOMAN'S ADVANTAGE

20 WOMEN ENTREPRENEURS show you
WHAT IT TAKES to **GROW YOUR BUSINESS**

MARY CANTANDO

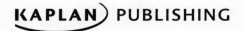
KAPLAN PUBLISHING

This publication is designed to provide accurate and authoritative information in regard to the subject matter covered. It is sold with the understanding that the publisher is not engaged in rendering legal, accounting, or other professional service. If legal advice or other expert assistance is required, the services of a competent professional should be sought.

President, Kaplan Publishing: Roy Lipner
Vice President and Publisher: Maureen McMahon
Acquisitions Editor: Karen Murphy
Senior Managing Editor: Jack Kiburz
Typesetter: Ellen Gurak
Cover Designer: Carly Schnur

Published by Kaplan Publishing,
a division of Kaplan, Inc.

Printed in the United States of America

06 07 08   10 9 8 7 6 5 4 3 2 1

Library of Congress Cataloging-in-Publication Data

Cantando, Mary.
  The woman's advantage : 20 women entrepreneurs show you what it takes to grow your business / Mary Cantando.
     p. cm.
  Includes bibliographical references and index.
  ISBN-13: 978-1-4195-3571-0
  ISBN-10: 1-4195-3571-4
  1. Women-owned business enterprises—Management. 2. Businesswomen. 3. Success in business. I. Title: Twenty women entrepreneurs show you what it takes to grow your business. II. Title.
  HD2341.C355 2006
  658.4'21082—dc22

                              2006002420

Kaplan Publishing books are available at special quantity discounts to use for sales promotions, employee premiums, or educational purposes. Please call our Special Sales Department to order or for more information at 800-621-9621, ext. 4444, e-mail kaplanpubsales@kaplan.com, or write to Kaplan Publishing, 30 South Wacker Drive, Suite 2500, Chicago, IL 60606-7481.

DEDICATION

John, after all these years, I'm still trying to figure out what I did to deserve you.

Keith, Suzanne, and Matthew, you are the triumphs of my life.

Foreword

I count it as a blessing and a privilege to know most of the women who share their wisdom in this book. Although these women all own multimillion-dollar—and in some cases billion-dollar—businesses, each of them has a wealth that goes far beyond dollars. This wealth reflects more than their financials and accumulation of titles, and it shines far beyond their prestigious customer lists and board positions.

The greatest wealth each of these women has achieved is her giving spirit. And it is that spirit that calls her to share what she has with others—whether that is her monetary resources, her time, or, importantly as in the case of this book, her wisdom.

The willingness of these women to reach out and provide guidance and support to other women entrepreneurs is an indication that no matter how far they've come, they remember the experience of getting started. And each of them wants to help you climb the ladder of entrepreneurial success by reaching down and extending her hand.

As women, we must all support each other in that climb.

Marsha Firestone, PhD
Founder and President, The Women Presidents' Organization
"Reaching Farther. Together"

Contents

Acknowledgments

My thoughts in this book arise from the amazing women I've worked with over 20 years. To acknowledge all those who influenced me would result in a list of thousands. So forgive me if I don't single you out on this page. I would, however, like to specifically thank some key women:

The Kaplan Publishing team: Karen Murphy, Eileen Johnson, Leslie Banks, Agnes Banks, April Timm, and Courtney Goethals. Thanks for helping me make it to the finish line.

Marsha Firestone and the facilitators and staff of the Women Presidents' Organization. Serving on your national board, facilitating WPO meetings, and being a part of the WPO sisterhood continue to enrich my life.

Members of the Charlotte and Raleigh WPO Chapters. We've shared amazing learning experiences and I thank you for your ongoing confidence in me.

Susan Bari and the members of the WBENC National Women's Forum. Your efforts make a real difference for women entrepreneurs everywhere.

My clients. Whether or not your story appears in these pages, it will always be written in my heart.

Cara DiSisto, Christina Wickson, Nicole Duncan, Carrie Monteleone, and Rachel Tunnicliffe, interns extraordinaire.

Patty Briguglio, Kipp Bodnar, and Gloria Lesher of MMI Associates, the best PR firm in the country.

Carol Nix of NIXdesign/Workin' Gal Cards.

Michele Lashley of Karacom Creative.

Monica Smiley of *Enterprising Women* magazine.
Karen Kerrigan of Women Entrepreneurs, Inc.
Sharon Hadary of the Center for Women's Business Research.

Introduction

Imagine a world where . . .

- you grow your business dramatically;
- you contribute to your clients, your employees, and your community; and
- you change the world.

My mission in writing *The Woman's Advantage* is to tell you, and women entrepreneurs around the globe, that such a world does exist.

One out of every 11 women owns a business, and each day 1,600 more start one. It's exciting to be a part of those numbers, but here's the challenge I see: Although millions of us own businesses, fewer than 5 percent of us generate more than $1 million in annual revenue. That statistic caused me to wonder: What do women do to get above $1 million? And how can more of us get there?

As I travel around the world, I meet women who have big dreams in their hearts but struggle to convert those dreams to reality. They can't cross the bridge from "a nice little business" to the flourishing world of multimillion-dollar entrepreneur.

The Woman's Advantage is here to lead you across that bridge.

For the past several years, I've worked exclusively with women entrepreneurs, and during that time I've noticed how our nurturing instinct compels us to share information and provide guidance to one another. Rather than competing, our nature calls us to cooperate. And I refer to this cooperative instinct as *The Woman's Advantage*.

This book taps into that advantage by capitalizing on my 20 years as an entrepreneurial executive and hundreds of years of experience from women who want to serve as your mentors. The book is organized into four sections that will enable you to:

1. Position your business for breakthroughs
2. Niche your business for influence
3. Certify your business for leverage
4. Market your business for growth

Each of these sections contains five chapters, and the format of each chapter is simple: I'll share a bit from my experience and then you'll learn from one of our 20 women entrepreneurs.

If you're looking for a theoretical, academic exercise, you've picked up the wrong book. What you're about to get is practical, roll-up-your-sleeves learning as self-made women show you how they built multimillion- and *billion*-dollar businesses.

I'm a self-taught businesswoman. I can't claim an MBA or Fortune 500 management experience. Because I stepped sideways into entrepreneurship, much of my thinking is a little unorthodox. The way I've developed my business would never be taught at Harvard or Wharton. But these approaches have worked for me and they work for my clients—women who own multimillion-dollar businesses.

You're about to learn some business concepts you may never have considered, like growing your business by "becoming famous" or cracking into Fortune 500 accounts by gaining certification for your business.

It took me a long time to figure out these things. The information was hard to find and I struggled to understand it. I don't want you to toil like I did. Over the past 20 years I've tried things—some worked and some didn't. But through it all I learned a lot. And that's what 20 women entrepreneurs and I are here to share with you: How to do things that we struggled to do.

I hope that these examples of how women, just like you, built multimillion-dollar businesses will open both your mind and your heart to this possibility. Each of these women generously steps forward to mentor you with just that goal. Their business expertise will capture your mind and their personal stories will capture your heart.

No matter how successful you are, you can travel the path to greater success, and that is what you'll gain from this book. That's my goal—to eliminate obstacles and smooth your path to business growth. I'm on a crusade, traveling the globe to create a perfect world for women entrepreneurs.

A world where . . .

- you grow your business dramatically;
- you contribute to your clients, your employees, and your community; and
- you change the world.

You're about to step into that world. Read on.

Position Your Business for Breakthroughs

Organizing Your Business for Growth

If you already own a multimillion-dollar business, congratulations! If not, you might run a small business. Or maybe you're just thinking about starting a business. Regardless of your current situation, the way you organize your business is the foundation for your success.

In many ways, growing a business is like raising a child. As an entrepreneurial mother, you have to plan for your business, guide it, and keep it healthy. Just as a mother has goals for her child, you probably have a vision of your business a few years down the line. And while it's fun to focus on the future, the success or failure of your business begins with the present—with how you organize your business for growth.

If you follow the ideas outlined here and the advice of your first mentor, Gloria Bohan, who built her one-person company into a billion-dollar business, you'll be well on your way to growing a business with The Woman's Advantage.

RESEARCH YOUR MARKET

As a business owner, you have a limited amount of time—168 hours a week. You don't get any more than that and neither do I. You also have a limited amount of energy and financial resources. So, the question is, how are you going to invest your time, energy, and money to earn the highest return?

Before investing money to start or expand a business, enter a new market, or develop a new product, it's important to be sure that customers need and are willing to buy your offering. You have to become familiar with the laws, demographics, customs, and competitors in your market and take the time to uncover potential sinkholes. And, as a woman entrepreneur, you should investigate whether or not to certify your business. (You'll learn all about that in Chapter 11.)

Research to Start a New Business

If you're starting a new business, look at the big picture and then break that down into small research projects. You'll want to consider issues such as target market, location, product or service offerings, staffing needs, and pricing in your research. Identify the areas where you need support, such as marketing, accounting, and legal issues, and identify resources to provide that support. Then bring all your information together to make your decision.

A fellow member of the Women Presidents' Organization, Erika Mangrum, owns Iatria Day Spas and Health Centers, an upscale chain of health-centered day spas. She actually came up with the idea for her business while getting a massage. When she discussed her idea with several people, she was met with enthusiastic response. But before jumping into it, Erika made her business the topic of her MBA thesis. To complete this study, she researched potential competitors, delved into legal and medical issues related to such an enterprise, explored pricing structures, and investigated available real estate. After careful study and the development of a detailed business plan, she located her first Iatria facility based on the results of her research. Now at the five-year point in her venture, Erika owns four Iatria Day Spas. And each time she opens a new one, she expands her research and capitalizes on what she has learned from her previous experience.

Research to Grow Your Current Business

If you're considering expansion, remember that existing markets almost always produce better results than new ones. You have a better chance of selling to existing customers and their acquaintances then to total strangers in a new market.

If you are going to expand, link from where you are to where you want to be in the future. Here's a case in point. One of my clients owns a dry-cleaning chain. After several years of success, she was looking for a fresh offering to generate additional revenue. She came to me with the idea of starting a doggy day care center. While this seemed like a feasible and certainly fun idea, I convinced her to back up and research the idea with her dry-cleaning customers. She did, and that research showed that her current customers weren't really interested in that new offering, but would pay a premium for shoe repair and tailoring. These offerings dovetailed much more smoothly with her existing dry-cleaning business, allowing her to grow her revenue without the risk and hassles of adding new facilities.

When organizing your business for growth always start with the research. Business is not about what you want to sell; it's about what the customer wants to buy. Period.

KEEP YOUR VISION ON THE VISION

Your vision is the keystone of your business. And a critical element of that vision is consistency. Here's an example. A few years back I envisioned a nationally renowned advisory firm that would help women grow their businesses. Besides being an author and consultant on this topic, I'm also a speaker and magazine columnist. So I was certainly positioned to achieve my goal. Yet, I found myself constantly taking side roads to chase revenue. While moving toward my vision I would be approached to speak or write a column on another topic. The dollar signs promised by those projects pulled me off course. I was making money and growing my business—but not in the direction of my dreams.

One day I discussed this with my daughter, Suzanne, and she cut to the chase, "Mom, if you're not turning down opportunities, then you don't really have a strategy." BINGO! I realized that although I claimed to have a vision, in fact I was always glancing away from it to chase revenue.

As a result of my epiphany, I developed a five-word vision: "National Expert on Women Entrepreneurs." I put this phrase at the top of my office whiteboard and every time I was presented with a speaking or writing or consulting opportunity, I glanced up at the board to see if it fit into my vision. As a result, I've turned down lots of individual opportunities in the past few years, but I have achieved my overall vision. And the revenue has followed.

Pamela O'Rourke, CEO of Icon Information Consultants, knew how to keep her eye on the ball when she started her business seven years ago. Pamela recognized that new accounts were critical to launching her business, so rather than taking a salary, she paid herself a commission. As a result, she couldn't afford to spend time on the fluff aspects of her business; she had to get out there and sell. Her personal compensation strategy focused her activities from the time she got up in the morning. The result? Seven years later, Pamela is running a $42 million business—and she still loves to sell!

DEVELOP YOUR STRATEGY

Strategy is the intersection of research and vision. Your strategy is your road map and you have to chart it out and stick to it to build a successful business. Your strategy will drive everything you do from whether you own or lease your space, to how you promote your business, to how you recruit your key employees.

Developing your strategy is not difficult, but it takes time and commitment. As a woman you should consider a strategy that dovetails with your personal life—that's the reason I run a home-based business these days rather than operating facilities all over the globe.

ADAPT AND GROW

It's pleasant to think that once your business is organized it will run day-to-day on autopilot. But business is about adapting. If you think back to the start of IBM, you might remember that it was a calculator company. From there it evolved into huge mainframe computers that were used solely by the government and corporations. The company next evolved to typewriters, followed by personal computers. After the recent sale of its PC business, IBM is, today, primarily a services company. So, even Big Blue, with its conservative business reputation, demonstrates that business success is about adapting to the market.

Let me tell you a great story about adapting for growth. One of my all-time favorite clients, Sheila Hale Ogle, owns MRPP, a business that buys media. Sheila's company purchases TV, radio, and print ads at bulk rates to provide the best value for her customers. For the past several years, these customers have clustered around two industries: hospitality and clinical studies organizations, the latter to advertise to those with asthma or diabetes or high cholesterol and have them enroll in drug-effectiveness studies. Like all of us, Sheila struggled following 9/11; as the hospitality industry tanked, major hotel chains slashed their advertising. Never one to panic, Sheila decided to focus on her clinical studies customers. But she didn't attack this opportunity in a conventional manner. No, she actually started a new clinical studies company to feed business to MRPP. She capitalized on her knowledge and connections in the clinical studies industry to create new revenue two ways—through her new company and by creating a new customer for her existing business.

So, like Sheila, you've always got to adapt to the market. But to do that effectively you can't spend your time putting out internal fires. You must have an infrastructure that supports your vision and strategy, and one that guarantees success in every customer interaction. Once you've got this organization in place, you're ready to adapt—ready to say, "Hmmm, how else can we grow?"

Starting or expanding a business is hard work, but it's not rocket science. Once you've determined your vision and strategy, you're halfway home. Millions of women across the globe own growing businesses. If they can do it, you can, too.

■ **MENTOR:**	*Gloria Bohan*
■ **BUSINESS:**	*Omega World Travel*
■ **LOCATION:**	*Fairfax, Virginia, U.S.A.*
■ **INDUSTRY:**	*Travel Agency*

On her honeymoon cruise aboard the Queen Elizabeth 2, with the love of her life—her husband, Dan—Gloria Bohan fell in love with something else: the travel business.

During the voyage, a friendly purser recognized the young couple as newlyweds and upgraded them to a better cabin. However, when they returned for a cruise the following year, they frustratingly lost out when the upgrades were offered instead to a group of travel agents on board.

Gloria complained about the situation to her husband, who replied, "If you can't beat 'em, join 'em," so the determined former schoolteacher took her life's savings and launched a one-person travel agency that ultimately became a billion-dollar international business.

Omega World Travel ranks as one of the biggest travel agencies in the world, with 200 offices and more than 1,000 employees worldwide, and the largest owned by a woman. Gloria has always touted the importance of diversity in business, and for her it's more than just words. Omega World Travel has been honored three times by Diversitybusiness.com as the "Top Diversity Owned Business."

In addition to the many awards her company has received over the years, Gloria herself receives continual recognition. She's been named "National Businesswoman of the Year" and "One of the Most Powerful Women in Washington," and has been enshrined in the Enterprising Women Hall of Fame.

Although Gloria's recognition as a successful woman entrepreneur is hard to match, she is much more than just an award-winning, high-profile CEO. Her philanthropic involvement includes Race for the Cure, the well-known cancer charity, and Suited for

Change, which provides career assistance for low-income women. And the former educator serves on the board of the Fairfax County Education Foundation, as well as that of her alma mater, Marymount Manhattan College.

As she looks to the future, Gloria's unique spirit of innovation and risk taking continues to drive her to new heights. Her attitude has always been "The sky's the limit," and she acted on that mantra quite literally by cofounding Space Adventures, whose mission is to send the first tourists into space.

HOW SHE DID IT

From early childhood, Gloria knew she wanted a career. When her family took weekend trips to New York City, she always pictured herself as a career woman walking along Fifth Avenue. She wanted the independence that working could bring.

When she launched Omega World Travel in 1972, she did whatever it took to find new business—from booking school bus trips to hosting free travel seminars. She knew she had to find a niche—something that the competition was not doing—and use that to make a difference. When the travel agency down the street closed at 5 PM, she stayed open until 7 PM. Every decision she made was focused on growth.

As a start-up business, Gloria knew that she had to seek out underserved markets. Wherever a customer expressed a need, she was ready to fill it. When clients asked her to provide service to new locations, she did. Within ten years, Gloria owned 15 travel offices. As she expanded beyond her initial small-town location, Gloria realized that the travel business was different from town to town and that no two customers were the same. She and her staff became aware of regional nuances and customized Omega Travel's solutions to meet local business needs.

As the business grew, Gloria continued to take risks. Under a test program, Omega World Travel was one of the first private businesses to competitively bid on official government travel. It was a chancy proposition because the prior contractor had defaulted and the airlines were reluctant to pay commissions on ticket sales. But, through vigilant billing practices, the relentless pursuit of a working arrangement with the airlines, and the enthusiastic support of government clients who recognized that Omega Travel offered better technology while cutting costs, the program became a success. Gloria knew then that she had found a niche in the travel business, and that niche was the U.S. government. And, because Omega Travel was based in the Washington, D.C., area, it was a natural fit.

Always looking for new opportunities, Gloria worked six days a week, sometimes seven, for almost two decades. Then she began to understand the potential of a strategically hired staff. As she organized her business for growth, she focused on hiring the right people for the right positions. By providing opportunities for advancement from within, she was able to empower her staff, generating loyalty and commitment, and giving them the confidence to excel.

How did Omega World Travel grow from one person to a billion-dollar organization? Gloria focused on organizing her business for growth. She never let herself become too satisfied. She kept reaching for new heights, new goals, as she continually worked to build a more efficient organization by streamlining processes and procedures.

As her small business grew into a million- and then a billion-dollar enterprise, Gloria was determined to remain knowledgeable about every aspect of the organization. She continued to take travel-related classes and worked alongside her staff at every level. As a result, she earned the respect of her employees because she understood their jobs, their struggles, and their needs, and she appreciated their roles in the organization.

Through the years, Gloria has learned to listen to her instincts. Omega World Travel has grown beyond Gloria's wildest dreams because she has recognized opportunity and listened to her heart when it told her to "Go for it!"

WHAT SHE ACHIEVED

The travel industry has undergone tremendous changes and faced great adversity in the past several years. Airline bankruptcies, terrorism, technology, and online booking are just a few of the factors that have impacted Omega World Travel. In her role as CEO, Gloria often feels like she's steering a roller coaster.

How does Gloria adapt to this constant change? Over the years, she's developed a "gearshift" philosophy that allows her to shift gears—or make changes—on a dime. Here's how she explains it, "In shifting gears, flexibility is paramount. You must know when to speed up to move to the front of the line or detour from your planned strategy because of an unanticipated event. A sensible business leader must look ahead for danger and slow down, perhaps even idle, until a roadblock clears and it's safe to proceed."

To adapt to the rapidly evolving travel industry, Gloria has closed some physical offices that were too costly, invested in new technologies, grown Omega Travel's meetings and incentives business, and demonstrated her progressive vision by supporting space tourism. And early on, Gloria embraced the Internet by offering clients their own travel reservation portals and becoming a major player in the online cruise booking industry.

Gloria made the critically important decision to capitalize on technology before most of her competitors did. Omega World Travel was one of the first agencies to use a computer reservation system and offer 24-hour customer service. Gloria pioneered the concept of on-site travel offices and electronic centralized billing and reporting for clients. As early as the mid-1990s, her company offered reservations via e-mail and voice recognition, and provided complete on-line booking by 1997. Omega Travel's progressive technology achievements enabled it to remain competitive with much larger travel agencies and eventually led to Gloria's decision to spin off the travel technology development into a separate company.

In the midst of this ongoing change, one thing remains constant in Gloria's life: her husband and biggest cheerleader, Dan. His creativity, business savvy, and inspiration have supported Gloria through the ups and downs of building a billion-dollar business, and Gloria is absolutely certain that she couldn't have achieved her success without him.

Omega World Travel is much more than just a business to Gloria; it's an everyday learning experience. Maybe it's the teacher in her, but she's developed a habit of grading herself on everything she does. "How am I adapting to change? Is my staff growing and learning new things, and how can I help? Am I continually exploring new opportunities? Are our customers happy?" All these things are important to Gloria and she's constantly assessing her progress.

Despite challenges, Gloria believes that the future is bright for female entrepreneurs who are willing to help others, adapt to change, and seek new opportunities. She feels our entrepreneurial zeal drives our success. And although we may fail at times, those failures move us along the path to achieving something special.

Asking Key Questions to Start and Grow Your Business

2

As a facilitator for the Women Presidents' Organization (WPO), I meet regularly with women dedicated to improving themselves and their businesses. One of the hallmarks of WPO is a round-table format developed by the Edward Lowe Foundation. Using this format, a member puts a problem or an opportunity on the table and her group asks rounds of questions that pave the way to a resolution. Because I've witnessed minor miracles as a result of this process, I've become a fan of asking good questions on an ongoing basis.

As you establish and grow your business, you can never ask too many questions.

ASK YOURSELF THESE PERSONAL QUESTIONS

Most of the women entrepreneurs I know want to do something important, not only for their customers and their employees, but also for their families and their communities. Oh sure, they're in business to make money, but the truly successful ones have seamlessly blended their businesses and their personal lives to create great results in both areas.

To achieve this blend effectively you must always be questioning what you're doing and how you're spending your time. Ask yourself these important questions about the fit between your business and your personal life:

- If I had to describe myself in a single phrase, what would that be?
- What values are most important to me?
- How do I reflect those values in my company?
- What is my personal mission in life?
- How does that mission dovetail with my business?
- Why did I start [am I starting] my business?
- Am I happy running my business?
- Am I fun to work with?
- What is creating stress in my life?
- What frightens me the most about my business?
- How do my personal weaknesses affect my business?

And, finally:

- What do I want to be remembered for?

ASK YOURSELF THESE BUSINESS QUESTIONS

After you've spent time thinking about your personal role, drill down to ask these questions about the challenges of your business:

- If I had to describe my company in a single phrase, what would that be?
- What's not working well in my business?
- What customer complaint am I ignoring?
- What do I need to do that I keep postponing?
- What external forces are shaping my industry?
- What is the lifetime value of my average customer? My biggest customer?
- What would happen to my business if I lost my biggest customer?

And, finally:

- What do I tolerate that I should change?

ASK YOURSELF THESE SALES QUESTIONS

Most people think sales questions are limited to those you ask during a sales call. But some of the most important sales questions are those you ask yourself about your sales.

Here are a few you should think about:

- What are five reasons a customer should do business with us?
- Who else can say that?
- What do our customers really buy from us?
- Are our offerings distinctive or are we like everyone else?
- What is our customer retention rate?
- What do we do to retain our customers?
- How do we respond to dissatisfied customers?
- Is our Web site current and well organized?
- What do people hate about doing business with our industry?
- How can we overcome that?
- Do we have all the information we need for every prospect and customer?
- How do we use that information to stay in touch? To increase sales?
- What is the yearly value of each customer? The lifetime value?
- How much of our sales budget do we invest to maintain our current customers?
- Who are our Top Five customers?
- How did we find and win those Top Five customers?
- How do we HONOR those Top Five customers?
- When did I last PERSONALLY interact with those Top Five customers?
- What is our competition doing to attract them and how close are they to leaving?
- What am I doing THIS WEEK to counter that?
- Who are our Top Five former customers?
- Why did they leave?
- What could I do THIS WEEK to win them back?
- How are we prepared for strategic sourcing?

- How often do we encounter reverse auctions?
- What is our strategy for handling these two fast-growing trends?

And, finally:

- Do our customers think we're fun to work with?

ASK YOUR STAFF ABOUT THESE ISSUES

Questions can be your most important management tool. As a business owner, you have the responsibility to ask the right questions, listen to the answers, and respond through appropriate words and actions. Before you ask these questions, determine how you'll use the answers, especially negative ones.

The worst thing you can do when you receive an answer you don't want to hear is to defend your position and make the employee feel uncomfortable. This is the recipe for preventing honest feedback from that employee and everyone he or she talks to.

Here are some questions you should ask your staff:

- If you had to describe our company in a single phrase, what would that be?
- What's the best thing about working for our company?
- What's the worst?
- What makes you proud of our company?
- If you were running this company, what would you do differently?
- If you could change one thing about me as the head of this company, what would it be?
- If you could change one thing about your job, what would it be?
- If you could change one thing about our products/services, what would it be?
- Who are our current and future competitors?
- What advantage do our competitors have?
- How can we overcome that advantage?
- How could we make more money?

- How could we save money?
- What do you see as the future of our industry?
- What should we do to prepare for or capitalize on that?

And, finally:

- How could we have more fun at work?

FIND OUT WHAT YOUR CUSTOMERS REALLY THINK

When you ask your customers for input, you're setting yourself up to hear the negative as well as the positive. When these negative comments rear their ugly heads, don't be defensive. Instead, thank your customer for the opportunity to correct the problem. Of course, it's always easier to listen to kudos, but to grow your business you've got to discover the negative and convert it to a positive.

Ask your customers these important questions to understand their relationships with your company:

- If you were to describe our company in a single phrase, what would that be?
- Why do you do business with us?
- What hard value do we bring to your company? What soft value?
- What does our competition provide that we don't?
- In what ways are we difficult to work with?
- What should we change about the way we do business?
- What other offerings can we provide to you now?
- What other offerings will you need from us in the future?

And, finally:

- What can we do to make your job easier?

MOVE FROM QUESTIONS TO OBJECTIVES

Once you identify the answers to these questions you're ready to assess your situation and move forward on your company's objectives.

■ **MENTOR:**	*Nikki Olyai*
■ **BUSINESS:**	*Innovision Technologies, Inc.*
■ **LOCATION:**	*Novi, Michigan, U.S.A.*
■ **INDUSTRY:**	*Information Technology*

ONE WOMAN WHO DID IT RIGHT

No one was surprised when Nikki Olyai received the U.S. Small Business Administration's Outstanding Women Entrepreneur Award in 2003. This was just another in a long string of awards she's amassed as president of Innovision Technologies, Inc., the engineering and information technology (IT) services company she founded in 1993. A dozen years after giving birth to her company, Nikki not only has a shelf full of awards but also a list of Fortune 500 companies and technology-driven U.S. government agencies such as NASA and the U.S. Department of Defense as clients.

Nikki received her master's in computer science from Oregon State University and began her career working for prestigious technology companies. From her first day on the job, Nikki always focused on asking questions—but not the superficial ones you might expect from a recent college grad. No, Nikki was always drilling down to find out "Why?" "How?" "What if?"

Always questioning, Nikki learned more and more about the software engineering industry, and her questions led her to realize a true need for software systems delivered in an effective and timely manner. From this realization, she asked the biggest question of her career, "What would it take for me to start my own business to deliver these systems?" And then, "Why not?" "How?" "How soon?"

Those initial questions were all answered when she launched Innovision Technologies, a company whose name reflects its goals—to leverage innovative technology to improve clients' businesses. Over the years, Nikki has built a team of engineers, IT specialists, and professionals led by a president who works alongside her fellow employees.

Nikki's industry is highly competitive, and she faces the daily challenge of working with ever-changing technologies. But by continually asking herself questions about every area of her business, she is able to stay one step ahead of her competition and provide exactly the solutions her clients need.

HOW SHE DID IT

Nikki built and grew a successful business by asking questions, not only of herself, but of her customers, her employees, and her vendors.

In the beginning, Nikki's questions were introspective, "Do I know what it takes to start a business? How about this business in particular? And, am I ready for it?" Since childhood, Nikki had always had an entrepreneurial spirit. So, when she could answer each of these questions successfully, she knew she was positioned to start her company. She had already developed her long-term business plan, was ready to make a large up-front financial investment, knew she could handle the responsibility of managing people, and understood that business success required personal sacrifices. So she made the commitment to move forward.

Her next step was to determine, "How will I build our team?" "What type of people do I want to work for me?" and "How will key employees fit into my business plan?" Hiring employees was an important step because Nikki wanted her company to be known for service excellence coupled with "nurturing" qualities. As she interviewed for key positions on her team, she sought unique qualifications that she knew only a select few possessed. She knew she'd be working intimately with these individuals and that they would have a strategic place in carrying out her plan, so every hiring decision was critical. Each employee would be charged with creating a lasting impression on clients by constantly exceeding their expectations.

The financial processes of starting a business were unfamiliar and challenging the first go-around and Nikki delved deeply into this area, knowing it was the downfall of many start-ups. Nikki asked herself these finance-related questions: "How will I address financial management systems and processes?" "How will banks evaluate my business?" And finally, "How do I develop a productive relationship with a financial institution?" Nikki's inquisitive nature led her to spend hours and hours asking the right questions to truly understand financial best practices.

Nikki knew that preparing to deal with the world of finance was a key to the success of her business. She understood the necessity of developing a "win-win" solution with a financial institution because her questions had helped her to understand how a bank was going to evaluate Innovision Technologies. She learned about the five Cs that financial institutions were looking for: character, capital, collateral, capacity, and condition. And she also learned that banks would evaluate her company's reputation, capital reserves, assets, and ability to repay any incurred debt. Being able to answer these key questions positioned her to present to the bank and obtain the funding she needed to start her business.

Feeling comfortable that she had asked all the right financial questions, Nikki's final area of questioning revolved around, "How am I going to acquire clients?" She knew that she had to create a viable customer base to build her business. She invested hours of research on this topic and ultimately created an "ideal client profile" by considering the current needs of prospective clients and again asking questions to determine what their future needs would be.

WHAT SHE ACHIEVED

As a result of Nikki's diligence in asking good questions, Innovision Technologies became an award-winning engineering and IT firm. And both the company and Nikki continue to be recognized. Nikki attributes much of her ongoing success to her ability to ask and answer key questions in a competitive business environment.

Innovision Technologies has grown significantly from its inception and its client base continues to grow. And through it all, Nikki never stops asking questions. A question she continually asks herself today is, "What will make Innovision Technologies special?" Nikki believes the answer to this question lies in the personal touch that many large companies are missing. So, in addition to providing state-of-the-art technology services, Nikki answers this question by ensuring her firm stands out through its personal and caring attitude toward clients.

Today, Nikki's company provides services to some of the world's largest corporations. Nikki has moved to this level by asking the right questions to build a strategic business plan, and then implementing all the components.

Innovision Technologies continues to operate at the leading edge of new technologies and constant change, and Nikki continues to be personally and technically innovative. In growing her business she continues to ask, "What's next?" Recently she answered that question by anticipating that her clients would require global capabilities. As a result, Nikki initiated a joint venture with the government of China. Through her business office in Shenyang, China, she is serving the Far East market, including China, Singapore, and Hong Kong, and she plans to continue to grow the global aspect of her business.

Nikki's most recent opportunity for new growth was her appointment of Innovision Technologies's new chairman and CEO, Dr. R. M. Jensen, who brings many years of leadership experience, a high level of expertise, and a reputation for excellence to the company. This strategic step came about as a response to Nikki's question, "How can we move to the next level within our industry?"

As an entrepreneur, Nikki prepared herself well for the challenges of starting her own company. She was driven by her personal values and she continues to stay true to them. She has a reputation of working around the clock to meet a deadline, and can always count on her team to support her efforts.

From the company's inception, Nikki, by asking key questions and taking the time to learn the answers, has given Innovision Technologies a competitive edge. As Nikki looks ahead she will continue to learn about the business world, her industry, and global expansion. She will always remain inquisitive because she knows that asking and answering the right questions have been a key to her past success and are instrumental to her future.

Establishing Objectives

3

I'm often surprised by the number of women who fail to set clear-cut objectives for their businesses. When I ask about their goals, I hear vague phrases about wanting to grow their business and needing more clients; but without specific objectives, their statements are really just wishful thinking.

Whether your business is large or small, establishing objectives is the only way to get from where you are to where you want to be. Specific, measurable objectives, coupled with an action plan to achieve them, move you forward. Setting these objectives will clarify priorities, eliminate confusion, and speed up progress. As a result you save time and money, reduce stress, and maximize your resources.

In building a business you set many objectives, but let's focus on the two that you can't run your business without: your team and your clients.

ESTABLISH OBJECTIVES TO CREATE YOUR TEAM

One of the most difficult, yet important, tasks you'll encounter in building your business is assembling a team to nurture and grow that business. Attracting a creative, ethical, hardworking staff on what might be a shoestring budget will be one of the toughest challenges you'll come across.

A friend of mine, Van Eure, owns a world-renowned restaurant called The Angus Barn. With a staff of more than 200, she has a crystal clear objective about hiring. It doesn't matter if she's hiring a chief financial officer or a dishwasher, Van's goal is always to hire as though she were building a "world-class" staff. As a result of this mind-set, it is no surprise that she has, in fact, assembled a world-class staff. Besides creating a team of employees who actually want to *serve* the customer, Van has a turnover rate that is 25 percent of the industry standard. In fact, she has employees who have been working with her for more than 40 years—and remember this is a restaurant! Van credits her success not only in hiring but in business in general to her objective of building a world-class staff.

Back in the late 1980s when we were building our technology services company, we used a cutting-edge development tool that took about six months to master. Because of the time required to learn this complex tool, I knew that employee turnover would destroy my bottom line, so I created what some considered an insane staffing objective: annual employee turnover of less than 5 percent.

Setting this stiff objective caused our human resources staff to be obsessive in their interviewing, testing, and reference checking. It also compelled everyone on our staff to be sure that new employees were set up to be successful. And it served as a reminder to me to take care of every employee every day. As a result of this obsession, we went for *four years* without loosing a *single* employee, and when the first finally did leave it was to follow a relocating spouse.

I believe that you can create a self-fulfilling prophecy about your team based on the objectives you set. So if your objective is to build a world-class team, guess what you build? And when your objective is to hire for minimal turnover, guess what happens?

ESTABLISH OBJECTIVES TO DEVELOP YOUR CLIENT BASE

No matter how good your product or service, you can't have a business without customers. Think about that. If you own a restaurant, you don't just serve food; you *feed customers.* If you own a travel agency, you don't book flights; you *make travel easy for customers.* And if you own a consulting company, you don't offer advice; *you help customers solve problems.*

Because your business can't survive without customers, some of your most critical objectives should revolve around developing your customer base. To do this, you want to create measurable goals for every important step of the sales process. I suggest that my clients work backwards to develop these objectives, which should include:

- Annual total revenue (existing clients and new clients)
- Annual revenue from new clients
- Number of new clients per month/quarter/year (depending on your offering and your sales cycle)
- Number of sales calls per month
- Number of new prospects per month
- Number of networking "touches" per month

You should also consider including objectives such as an annual client retention rate. And here's an idea: Remember what happened when I set my employee turnover rate at 5 percent? I ended up with zero. What would happen if you set your client retention rate at 100 percent? And if you were serious about that goal, suppose you provided everyone in your company with a year-end bonus if you achieved it. Do you think that you and your staff would handle clients any differently with that mind-set than you are doing now? And what kind of a difference would that make to your bottom line?

Here's a great example of how client development goals can dramatically impact your business. Barb Sheridan is president of HR XCEL, a multimillion-dollar firm that provides outsourcing of human resources and benefits administration. Barb's firm had been selling only in the southeastern United States and she wanted to expand geographically to cover the entire country, so she established two client development goals:

1. Brand the company name nationally on the Web, focusing on search engines.
2. Align the company with specific national distribution partners, including health insurance brokerage and consulting firms.

As a result of focusing on these objectives, HR XCEL expanded dramatically, with new major clients from New York City to California. As an added benefit of Barb's goal to align with distribution partners, these firms now refer their clients to HR XCEL.

ESTABLISH OBJECTIVES BASED ON THE STAGE OF YOUR BUSINESS

It's important to base your objectives on your stage of business and to evolve those objectives as your business grows. And, of course, your goals must be measurable (how many new clients? by what date?) and realistic (can we REALLY obtain that number of new clients?).

Here's what objectives based on business stage might look like.

Develop Objectives to Start a Business

If you're just starting your business, you should develop objectives to:

- Conduct research to determine the offerings customers will buy
- Build solid relationships with prospects, customers, vendors
- Establish facility
- Build staff
- Launch offerings
- Promote offerings
- Reach profitability

Brooke Billingsley knows firsthand that setting objectives yields tremendous results. Eight years ago, she launched Perception Strategies, Inc., from the humble setting of her spare bedroom. Brooke knew her target audience of hospitals and health care systems would greatly benefit from Perception's health care mystery shopping, but presenting a new service concept was a daunting task.

Brooke embraced the challenge and created specific goals beginning with Perception's corporate *perception*.

Working on her goals one by one, Brooke created a professional image through expertly designed logos, Web site, phone lines with voice mail, and high-quality marketing materials; she specifically avoided any impression of a "home-based business."

Next, she focused on the company's profit margins. She set sales goals to reach profitability and then grow her business by $100,000 annually. She positioned Perception to achieve those goals by increasing the staff and moving to a formal office space, both the result of previously set objectives. Based on her plans, the company outgrew that space and Brooke saw the profitability of *purchasing* the company's next office space, which she did.

So, after eight years of objectives that have driven eight years of growth, Brooke continues to set her sights high with a current $5 million sales goal and planned hiring of 16 additional staff members.

Develop Objectives to Grow a Business

Once you enter the growth phase of your business, your objectives might include:

- Launch additional offerings
- Expand to new markets
- Increase staff
- Enlarge your client base
- Grow revenue and profitability

When Patty Briguglio, owner of MMI Associates, decided to expand her award-winning marketing and public relations firm from Phoenix to Raleigh, she was not concerned that MMI become the biggest firm in her new market, but that it was one of the best. Patty's expansion objective was to build a client base of multimillion-dollar, privately held, entrepreneurial companies.

In deciding which companies to pursue, Patty set specific objectives to target those with accessible, central decision makers who understood the value of PR and would allow MMI to take the lead. Patty chose her clients with care and went all out to excel for them.

As she met her objectives for obtaining new clients, Patty fulfilled the corresponding objectives of expanding her staff and office facilities to service them. By creating very specific objectives she was able to build profitable long-term relationships with high-profile clients and grow her business dramatically.

Develop Objectives to Maintain a Growing Business

To maintain business growth, you should develop objectives to:

- Build an executive team
- Continue to launch additional offerings
- Maintain and expand your client base
- Continue to expand staff
- Continue to grow revenue and profitability

Sharon Evans, CEO of Fort Worth–based CFJ Manufacturing, believes if you set good objectives to *start* and *grow* your business, you will have no trouble establishing the objectives you need to *maintain* that growth. In many cases, that simply means continuing to do whatever it took to get you where you are—whether it is launching additional offerings, hiring additional staff, or growing revenue—while always keeping an eye toward potential challenges.

As a provider of total recognition award programs, Sharon has driven CFJ to double-digit annual growth for several years running. And she's achieved that growth by focusing on her current client base. While she does have goals for acquiring new clients, Sharon really keeps her eye on CFJ's specific objectives for maintaining and growing existing clients. As a result, prospects are impressed by Sharon's large number of repeat customers. The upshot is credibility and steady growth both from existing clients as well as new ones.

Sharon believes you must stay focused and set your ongoing objectives to reflect your initial goals. A key element of these objectives is continuing to hire and train reliable employees to support the areas of your business that are growing. But beyond hiring reliable individual employees, Sharon's most important business objective is to maintain an executive team that shares her vision but is not afraid to disagree with her on individual decisions.

Sharon has learned that always keeping her eye on her key objectives—maintaining existing clients, hiring and training reliable employees, and building a stellar management team—is what it takes to maintain a growing business.

■ **MENTOR:**	*Cristiana Panicco*
■ **BUSINESS:**	*Sorrento Lingue*
■ **LOCATION:**	*Sorrento, Italy*
■ **INDUSTRY:**	*International Language School*

ONE WOMAN WHO DID IT RIGHT

Cristiana Panicco is on a mission to change the meaning of one word: visionary—or rather *visionario* in Italian.

Born and raised in a small town near Torino, Italy, Cristiana is fluent in English, French, German, and her mother tongue, Italian. Because she has always been passionate about sharing the beauty of her Italian language and heritage with others, Cristiana established an international language school in the charming city of Sorrento in southern Italy. There she created not just a school, but an international community where both Italians and internationals alike come together to interact and exchange their culture, ideas, and perspectives.

Although she is a successful entrepreneur, Cristiana still must contend with significant cultural bias as an Italian woman. In Italy, a woman with lofty goals is mockingly referred to as a *visionario*. In cultures outside of Cristiana's, the term *visionary* is one of the highest compliments that can be paid to an entrepreneur. In Italian, however, this word describes a person with mystical visions or hallucinations—someone who imagines things that do not exist.

Thus, Cristiana is on a mission to change the meaning of a visionary within her culture by creating a thriving business out of what began as a mere dream.

Cristiana's goal is for Sorrento Lingue to be the premier center for international education and language studies. But as any successful entrepreneur knows, great business ideas begin by defining exactly what you want to accomplish. Success is achieved by establishing objectives.

HOW SHE DID IT

When Cristiana first opened the doors of Sorrento Lingue in 1998, her goal was to share the Italian language and culture with individuals from all countries of the world. And she set her objectives to accomplish just that. As she began to reach these objectives, Cristiana discovered that there was also significant demand for teaching foreign languages to Italians. As she explored this opportunity, she realized that it could become a viable offering and provide a significant stream of revenue; so she established goals to build that offering as a separate element of her business.

As a result, Sorrento Lingue began to teach English to school-age children as well as to individuals at major corporations in the area. And it also began offering English, Spanish, French, and German to all the hotels within the Sorrentina Peninsula region. As Cristiana accomplished each of these goals, she set new ones to position her business for further exciting opportunities.

Cristiana has always felt that success in setting objectives arises from three characteristics:

1. *Determine your passion.* When Cristiana identified an objective or was presented with an opportunity, she first asked herself: "How do I feel about this? Am I passionate? Do I really want to achieve this goal?" When the answer was yes, she moved straight to the next step . . .
2. *Refine your objective.* Cristiana focused each goal by thinking about it objectively and writing down exactly what she wished to achieve. Then she consulted with others to further refine her idea. Once she had developed a clear objective, she moved to the final step . . .
3. *Plan for success.* To achieve her goals, Cristiana focused on resources and scheduling. She analyzed available resources such as staffing and facilities and decided on a realistic time frame for achievement.

While building Sorrento Lingue, Cristiana constantly thought of new ideas and objectives; however, she found that it was nearly impossible to recall all of these ideas without writing them down. So she developed the habit of carrying what she calls a "go anywhere, anytime" document where she recorded all her ideas, no matter how random.

She then set aside time to review that document and categorize each idea according to distinct areas of her business. Some might fall into the area of marketing, while others might be new business opportunities. Cristiana believes that the key to achieving goals is to have a starting point, and her starting point is simply writing down every idea as it pops into her head. From there she shapes it into a goal.

Once Cristiana developed a goal, she determined *how* she was going to achieve it, *when* she would achieve it, and after accomplishing it, she judged *how well* she had achieved it.

For example, one of Cristiana's key goals at Sorrento Lingue was to increase student enrollment within a specific time frame by a particular percentage. By establishing exact criteria, such as dates and percentages, her team was able to assess their success. It was important for them to know the student count at the start of the project and to calculate the number of additional students required to achieve their goal. This allowed them to establish strategies to achieve this goal and to set time frames throughout the project to assess how they were doing.

Besides actually achieving her goals, one of the highlights for Cristiana in setting objectives is the excitement and pride of her staff when they reach their goals.

WHAT SHE ACHIEVED

When Cristiana first started Sorrento Lingue, she tried to do everything herself—from answering phones to teaching to marketing, right down to cleaning the school. Eventually, she realized that this level of activity was preventing her from accomplishing her goals. She decided that she needed to make immediate changes. First, she had to trust her staff. And second, she had to share her goals and objectives for Sorrento Lingue with them and involve them in achieving those goals.

Cristiana found that once she shared these goals with her staff and made them part of the process, they felt a sense of ownership. As a result, the team was able to achieve the goals more quickly and efficiently than she would have achieved them herself. She also noticed an unexpected benefit—an increase in pride within the Sorrento Lingue family.

Because Cristiana had spent so much time developing and working on her dream, she was initially reluctant to share it. She worried that someone else might not perform a task as well as she would. However, her most empowering moment occurred when she realized she could trust her staff and that each of them had specific qualities and skills that together would fulfill the goals she had set for the school.

When individuals decide to attend Sorrento Lingue, they are enrolling not only to learn a language but to open themselves up to a completely new experience—engaging with people they would not otherwise engage with, dining on food they would not normally eat, living with a family from a different culture, and learning about subjects they had not previously considered. The underlying objective of Sorrento Lingue is to break down barriers—enabling individuals regardless of culture, age, race, gender, or profession, to share a fulfilling cross-cultural experience.

As she looks to the future, Cristiana knows she will continue to set goals for both Sorrento Lingue and for herself. She plans to continue attending international conferences and meeting other successful women, as well as sharing her experiences with young entrepreneurs to inspire them to set and achieve their goals. And beyond her goals for the school itself, Cristiana recently achieved another of her long-term goals—publishing an Italian language resource book.

Cristiana doubts that her craving for knowledge will ever be satisfied. As she experiences new ideas, she is determined to share what she has learned not only with women, but with all members of the Italian community. Cristiana is a true visionary and she is on a mission to show her compatriots the value of that. She is on a mission to change the meaning of *visionario*.

Understanding
Your Value to the Business

4

What legacy do you want to leave? Besides making money and having fun, what other reasons do you have for running your own business?

We all make choices in life, and if you want to make a real difference—if you want to leave a legacy—you need to control how you invest your time. This all comes down to making choices.

UNDERSTAND YOUR VALUE

So many areas of your business spin at the same time: finance, marketing, lead generation, sales, product/service fulfillment. With all these considerations, it's no wonder that some women get stuck just working, working, working. Because so many of us start our careers in the field or front line, when we move to running our own businesses, we often find it difficult to step back and delegate the actual work. We find ourselves ordering office supplies or proofing the marketing materials or running to the post office instead of assigning these tasks to a staff member.

To succeed in business, you must understand your value to the organization. Your responsibility is to focus your time on actions that contribute the greatest value to your business and to delegate any activities that others can do.

Here's one approach. When I was running a multilocation business, I thought of sales, production, and service delivery each as a separate box. As I opened a new location, I created each of those boxes and then figured out how to step out of them. Stepping out involved two tasks: first, identifying a key manager to step into each box, and then ensuring that everyone knew I no longer resided in that box. This worked well for my remote locations, because I wasn't physically present most of the time. But in my main location where I had been running things for years, employees bypassed their new managers and continued to come to me for answers and direction. So I decided to move to a home office and run my primary location as though it were a remote office. This unorthodox solution allowed me to use my time appropriately to focus on the big picture, and allowed the managers to maintain ownership of their areas of the business.

To capitalize on your entrepreneurial strengths, you've got to learn to delegate so you can spend your valuable time strategizing and leading rather than doing.

CAPITALIZE ON YOUR PASSION

Passion is one trait shared by all those who make a difference. If your business is well run and profitable, then you have more time to indulge in your passions. Although your business may be your most driving passion, you are more than just the owner of a company. You may be a mother, spouse, sibling, aunt, friend, community volunteer, and more. When you make time for the passions that revolve around those other roles you become a better business owner as well.

One of my most cherished roles is that of grandmother. And one of my favorite activities is attending my grandchildren's sporting events. I've been known to cut a business trip short to get to Megan's soccer game or get up at 3 AM to finish a project so I don't miss Alex's baseball game. These activities, and others such as meditating, working out, and just taking my Yellow Lab for a walk, have the power to invigorate me so I can run my business with a clear head.

What about you? Your friends and family need you in their lives. And your business needs a leader who lives a well-rounded passionate life.

TAKE CARE OF YOURSELF

A positive attitude and healthy lifestyle are key elements of business success because enthusiasm and vitality are powerfully attractive; they draw people to you and make you successful.

I really take care of myself. I eat very sensibly (too sensibly, according to my husband, who would love to find chocolate chip cookies in the pantry) and I work out regularly. Do I always feel like working out? No. More often than not, I'd rather sit at my computer than go to the gym. But to stay motivated, I've convinced myself that for every day I work out I add a day to my life. If you do the math, you'll see that's a pretty good return on investment: 1 hour for 24.

I've developed a habit of spending time only on things that make me happy or drive revenue. I know some women entrepreneurs who, although they hate cooking and can clearly afford to have someone do it for them, rush home from their business every evening to make dinner. And then they complain about it! Why would you spend your valuable time doing something that you don't enjoy that doesn't generate revenue?

Look at it this way: Every minute you invest in doing something that a male competitor is not doing, you put yourself at a competitive disadvantage. So if you like cleaning the office break room, by all means do it; but if not, pay someone to do it. The same goes for wrapping holiday gifts or unpacking office supplies. Every minute you spend on tasks like that creates an advantage for your competition.

The flip side of that, however, are the important tasks that you may not want to do but really can't delegate. Things like playing golf with a customer even if you don't like to play golf. Or calling an irate client. Or reprimanding a direct report. I always dreaded dealing with these kind of things until my friend, Carol Lindell, owner of DCI Home Resource, taught me a nifty trick. The first thing in the morning, Carol does three important things that she doesn't want to do. She gets them out of the way and then enjoys the rest of her day. I've implemented Carol's approach and it makes a difference in my whole day. Give it a try.

MAKE AN IMPACT

As a woman entrepreneur your business is a reflection of you. This puts you in a position to make a positive impact on your staff and your customers. A recent business school study determined that a positive attitude is 93 percent more important to success than intelligence, skill, and information combined. That's a pretty clear indication of the value of attitude.

But let's face it. Sometimes it's tough to be positive. However, if you consider all the gifts you've been given, you've got a *responsibility* to be as upbeat as possible. Terry Espy, owner of The Momentum Group, is a cancer survivor. Whenever someone starts to woefully discuss their problems with her, she smiles and wisecracks, "Well, heck, it's not *cancer!*"

But sometimes is it just that—cancer, or maybe something that's devastating to your business. How do you respond to that? Over the years I've developed an approach that I call "Three Good Things." Here's how it works: Whenever something goes wrong, I challenge myself to find three good things about the situation. I remember right before the dotcom bust, one of our telecommunications clients canceled a project that was utilizing 24 dedicated employees. I really struggled to find three good things about this situation. As I considered it, I thought, Well, the client *has* committed to paying the outstanding invoices. And we can move half of those people to another project. And this will give me the opportunity to eliminate a few individuals who have been less than A Players. While my approach may seem simplistic and Pollyanna-like, it always works for me. No matter how tough the situation, you can always find three good things about it.

Impact Your Employees

There's no question that Walt Disney was a brilliant entrepreneur. When planning Disney World, he directed that Cinderella's castle be the first thing built, so that its tall spires could be seen by the workers combating the sweltering heat, incessant mosquitoes, and marshy swamplands. Disney knew that actually seeing the vision of what they were building would move his team forward with intensity.

How about you? What is *your* castle? Is it visible to your employees?

Along these lines, I've noticed a trend among women entrepreneurs that I refer to as "Crafting a Celebration." More and more women demonstrate their commitment to their employees by creating handmade crafts. For example, Marcie Broga36

n, owner of Brogan & Partners Convergence Marketing, paints and personalizes a little red chair for each employee's child; this is her way of saying that there is always a place for every child to come and visit. And Lana Calloway, owner of Exhibit Resources, hand-stitches a quilt to celebrate each employee's wedding or new baby, and she presents it at a companywide shower. Yet another woman takes a picture of each employee doing something outside of work, such as playing tennis, planting a garden, or coaching a youth sports team. She then mats and frames each picture and adds it to her "Real People Gallery" in the company's lobby. This "Crafting a Celebration" trend allows women entrepreneurs to share in their employees' lives by crafting a labor of love.

Impact Your Community

Your business is successful as part of a community and that community has needs that only you can fill. Whether for a professional organization, chamber of commerce, or your children's school, your time, energy, and ideas are vital.

By taking on a leadership role, you have an opportunity to impact your community and leave a legacy. Look around and see what cause motivates you—what contribution you can make. As a woman entrepreneur, you are in a unique position to make a real difference. Don't miss the opportunity.

Impact Your World

Here's how I see my impact on the world: I help women grow their businesses. As those businesses grow, employees are hired. Those employees are then able to care for their families by spending money in their community. As money is spent in the community, more jobs are created.

My impact has a ripple effect. I never know where it ends, but I absolutely trust that I am making a difference in the world. I am the only person in the world able to run my company to produce my specific result. And so are you.

■ **MENTOR:**	*Janice Bryant Howroyd*
■ **BUSINESS:**	*ACT-1 Group*
■ **LOCATION:**	*Torrance, California, U.S.A.*
■ **INDUSTRY:**	*Staffing, Human Resources, and Management Solutions*

ONE WOMAN WHO DID IT RIGHT

Janice Bryant Howroyd will never forget her mother-in-law's advice, "Your children will pay more attention to what you *do* than what you *say*." Since starting ACT-1 in 1978, Jan has applied that philosophy not only to her children but to her customers, employees, associates, and friends. In fact, she has built her profitable multimillion-dollar, California-based business on that simple belief— doing what you say you will do.

Raised in rural North Carolina, a state whose motto is "To *be* rather than to *seem*," Jan learned early on that life was not about appearance but about authenticity. And over the years, she crafted this concept into a personal mantra of what is important to her: "God, family, country, and company."

Even today, while she sits at the top of one of the largest privately held companies in the world, Jan has stayed close to God, never compromising her standards to gain revenue. As she travels the world, far from her rural roots, she remembers and cherishes her humble beginnings as 1 of 11 children. And motivated by the memories of her youth, she still recognizes home and family as her source of refuge from running a staffing and workforce technology empire.

Since the beginning, Jan has built her business without compromise. Relying on patience, common sense, and hard work, she's crafted ACT-1 into an internationally recognized firm. And in return for all she's accomplished, Jan now focuses much of her energy on giving back to the local, national, and international community. From her days as a little girl in rural North Carolina, she learned about crop rotation and understood the concept of returning nutrients to the soil. To keep her world fertile, Jan knows that she can't just take without giving back. So she gives back constantly to her employees, her customers, and her community. And she gives the best she's got to offer.

HOW SHE DID IT

In 1978, Jan combined $967 in personal savings with a $533 loan from her mother to lease a small office with a desk and a single phone. Using the initial profit from her fledgling business, Jan wrote her first check—in repayment to her mother. Before long, she expanded to two locations and then five. Today ACT-1, with corporate headquarters in Torrance, California, has locations and customers around the world. However, Jan never considers her business in terms of numbers but in terms of people, and that's been the secret to her achievement.

From the beginning, Jan understood that her success depended on individual people—on the capabilities of every single employee she placed. From the outset, she felt so strongly about the abilities of her temporary workers that she offered to return a customer's money if an ACT-1 employee didn't prove to be everything Jan had promised. With her total profit on the line every day, Jan relied on her business skills and intuition to place the right person in the right environment. And she learned that her value to the business rested in her personal relationships with both applicants as well as customers.

Although Jan can't begin to know every one of the 65,000+ individuals working under the current banner of ACT-1, she does continue to invest her personal time and energy to ensure that her management team is entrepreneurial in spirit but intrapreneurial in vision. Over the years, she's focused on hiring key staff who would work as though ACT-1 was their own company but always keep her mission and vision at heart. "Leaders who are willing to take out the trash" is how Jan describes her leadership team.

Although building an operation as large as ACT-1 would have overwhelmed most women, Jan took it a day at a time, and every morning she expected that day to be even more exciting than the last. As a result of her enthusiasm for the business, Jan never felt that she needed to "escape" from ACT-1; she never felt that she needed to get away from her work to enjoy life. A highly spiritual individual, Jan always felt that her work was her meditation—that it brought inspiration to her life.

As her business grew, Jan realized that her community was growing as well. She began to understand that her community had expanded beyond her business, her city, her industry, and even her beloved family. She realized that the entire world was now her community. And she understood that she was in a position to impact others throughout the world. She saw her power as a vehicle to address racism and sexism. Through her own personal power, Jan demonstrated just how far an African-American woman could go. She showed others that hiding behind "labels" and using them as excuses for failure would not move you ahead. She demonstrated over and over again how much one individual could achieve when she stepped from behind the labels and the excuses.

A proud alumna of North Carolina A&T University, Jan had been taught from an early age that "education is the road to freedom." One day, after she had closed a particularly large contract, Jan realized that she could use the profit from that contract to provide a college scholarship for a young black woman, and that thought made her heart leap. While writing that first scholarship check, Jan realized the awesome power she held; she could change someone's entire world by providing the freedom of education. She understood the opportunity that she had been given to free others and, to this day, she continues to provide scholarships and *freedom* to deserving students.

WHAT SHE ACHIEVED

Over the years, Jan has found that the best way to impact her business is to live by her personal creed. It is important for her to show not only her staff, but her customers and her community, that she has integrity—that she actually does what she says she's going to do. As a result they believe and trust in her.

It is difficult for Jan to think of her business without her family. From her early childhood, Jan's mother served as the role model who lit the path for her. From her mother, Jan learned of the importance that family plays in life, and she counts herself lucky to have family members who are also strong businesspeople. Currently, eight members of her family, many with engineering degrees, serve on the staff of ACT-1.

As she moves forward, Jan shares the goals of every woman entrepreneur—to run and grow a profitable company. And she shares the goals of every mother—to enable her children to lead fulfilled lives. Jan is excited about how her daughter, Katharyn, a graduate of USC, and son, Brett, a university student, might move forward. It's possible that they may become a part of ACT-1 or their experience and success may inspire them in another business. But Jan doesn't intend to just "give" them a leadership position in her company; although they are competent and capable, she expects them to earn their way toward ACT-1 leadership.

Over the years, Jan has grown ACT-1 from a temporary staffing company to an international organization with four key verticals: core staffing, technical placement, government, and technology. In devising this structure, Jan insists that each vertical be successful in its own right and also work with the others to achieve the greatest synergy for her company. When Jan hires key individuals for any of these verticals, she requires that they have expertise in the specific vertical, but also understand the value of the organization as a whole.

So what kind of a legacy does a woman like Janice Bryant Howroyd intend to leave? Well, so far, the little girl from rural North Carolina has developed a multimillion-dollar business, a strong, loving family, and a proven commitment to making a difference in the world. And that should be enough for any one woman. But beyond that, Jan is passionate about continuing her legacy of noncompromising service to every ACT-1 customer and applicant. And despite her success, status, and prominence in the business world, she gets up every morning fired up about going to work to fulfill this legacy.

Instilling Confidence

5

Developing the confidence of your employees, customers, prospects, and vendors is critical to your business success, and this confidence is more important today than ever. Over the years, I've learned that four primary components are necessary for instilling confidence: responsibility, reliability, relationships, and references.

INSTILL CONFIDENCE THROUGH RESPONSIBILITY

When building your organization, it's important you are viewed as an individual with something of real value to offer.

As a woman entrepreneur, you have a real advantage, because you *are* your business. When you sell *your* product, *your* service, *your* company, in effect you are selling *yourself*. So it's natural for you to believe 100 percent in what you're doing and what you're selling.

Let's look at that a little deeper.

Most women entrepreneurs have both a personal mission and a business mission; and in the best cases, these missions are tightly interwoven. For example, Dr. Angela Bayliss, a chiropractor who also provides holistic health care services, has a personal mission to help others enjoy their lives. In her business, she actually focuses very little on "making money" and almost entirely on her business mission of enabling others to enjoy healthy, pain-free lives. So in the process of blending her personal and business missions, she's developed a thriving business that actually does make a lot of money. Because she is 100 percent committed to what she is doing—helping others—her business just seems to grow without effort.

If you don't have this strong sense of responsibility, purpose, and commitment about your business, if you don't believe that what you're doing in some way helps others, then I encourage you to reconsider the business you're building, because if you can't demonstrate 100 percent commitment to your mission, you won't have much success in selling it.

INSTILL CONFIDENCE THROUGH RELIABILITY

About a dozen years ago, when I was running an IT services firm, I assigned one of my graphic artists to design a T-shirt as a holiday gift. I asked her to take our company name, "PDR," and conduct a contest among our clients to develop a phrase, starting with those letters, which represented a client's view of our company.

The winning submission, which came from a client named Joan, still brings a smile to my face. It's a caricature of a cowboy in spurs wearing a ten-gallon hat. And beside him are three words starting with the letters P-D-R: "Purdy Dadgum Reliable."

What makes this phrase so great is the fact this is truly how Joan felt about our organization: that we were reliable, that we would deliver what she needed, when she needed it, no matter what.

Thinking back on my experiences in selling to Joan, I realize that after we completed our first project for her, I never really had to sell to her again. In effect, all I did was take her next order. That doesn't mean that we didn't have competition; every IT consulting firm in the state was vying to work for this Fortune 50 company. In fact, our biggest competitor consistently underbid us on proposal after proposal, but somehow we always won the contract because Joan was so convinced of our reliability.

As Joan referred more and more of her colleagues to us, our reputation for reliability spread. We began winning contracts with other divisions of her company, and then with other of their sites around the world.

I can't think of a thing that I've done in building any business that has had more of an impact on revenue than just taking care of clients like Joan—just being sure that what we delivered was "right" every single time. Just being "Purdy Dadgum Reliable."

INSTILL CONFIDENCE THROUGH RELATIONSHIPS

Tana Greene, CEO of Strataforce, really understands the value of relationships. Although her company has grown to more than 2,000 employees, she still insists on meeting with every one of her major clients on a quarterly basis. But she's created a little twist to these meetings.

At the beginning of each meeting, Tana and her management team meet with the client's management team to discuss reports, productivity, and future plans. Then Tana asks her team to leave the room and she sits alone with the client and asks the question, "Now tell me the truth, how is everything *really* going?"

While some may shudder at the idea of inviting such frank and undiluted feedback, Tana says this one simple question is the linchpin of her success in business—and in life.

"All we really have are relationships—with employees, clients, and everyone we cross paths with," Tana says. "Those relationships must be open and honest to ensure that everyone benefits fully. Only by approaching others with a real desire to understand what they are feeling, facing, or uncertain about, can we be sure that we're holding up our end of the bargain."

A successful business leader, involved community leader, mother, and wife, Tana says her accomplishments have all radiated from this same, seemingly simple approach to honoring relationships. She says she learned early on that it wasn't so much who you knew but how well you knew them. As a result, Tana tends to find herself carrying on open and in-depth interactions with everyone from neighbors to strangers, family members to clients.

But no group tends to invite as many of Tana's questions as her own employees. When Tana decided to leave her successful franchise business behind and start Strataforce, her first priority was to build a cohesive team. To do so she recruited old associates as well as new talent—slowly assembling a group to help guide and grow the fledgling company.

And grow it they did. In just its third year of business, Strataforce has quickly expanded from a small, single location to a decorated industry leader with five offices. Yet even as the company has grown, Tana has shown an unprecedented knack for retaining not only clients but employees as well.

This, again, may well go back to that one simple relationship question Tana frequently poses—and so fervently believes in. Half mantra, half question: "Now tell me the truth, how is everything *really* going?"

INSTILL CONFIDENCE THROUGH REFERENCES

I'm not sure where the idea of distributing testimonial letters came from, but as far as I'm concerned they don't carry much weight. Just think about it, have you ever read a bad one?

Although I don't put much weight on testimonial letters, I know firsthand that references can add tremendous value to credibility. So rather than providing standard testimonial letters, I create Client Profiles, which I make available during the sales process.

Here's how this works.

I show the prospect a master listing of all my client references, including:

- The organization's name, address, and industry
- A listing of the company's products or services
- A profile of the services I've provided to that client and the results we've achieved working together

From this master listing, the prospect selects the three individuals with whom she would like to speak. When she makes her selection, I hand her an individual Client Profile sheet for each of these clients. Each sheet contains more details and the client's name and contact information. The prospect is then free to contact these clients.

People tell me that the real value of these Client Profiles is the flexibility they feel when selecting from a collection of clients, rather than having client testimonials thrust upon them. Prospects typically select individuals from similar industries, and hearing about their success in working with my company underscores their confidence.

This is what ultimately causes them to come on board as clients.

BRING IT ALL TOGETHER

So there you have it—the four components that build confidence in a business and in you as a business leader: responsibility, reliability, relationships, and references.

Before we leave these four confidence builders, I want to show you a simple e-mail that perfectly ties them together. In 2005, in the aftermath of a devastating hurricane, Annette Taddeo, CEO of LanguageSpeak, a Miami-based translation company, sent the following personalized e-mail to her clients, vendors, and colleagues:

> Dear Mary,
> On behalf of LanguageSpeak, I'd like to give you an update on our recovery from Hurricane Wilma. First and foremost, all the LanguageSpeak team, family, and loved ones are safe and sound. Our disaster planning went into full force prior to the hurricane. We ensured that our ongoing projects were still being worked on by our translation teams outside South Florida. Within 24 hours of the storm, our Miami headquarters was fully operational thanks to our carefully designed recovery plan, which included backup generators and backup IT systems. We are ready and able to help you with any language project you may have. As always, thank you for your business and understanding.
> Saludos,
> Annette

I was in awe when I received this e-mail from Annette, because in a single paragraph she sent a solid message of confidence. *Relationships* are most important and our people are safe. You can *rely* on us to take care of your projects in a safe location. We're *responsible* enough to have a recovery plan. Although our *references* are implied, this e-mail demonstrates that our clients are important.

If Annette can instill confidence four ways in a one-paragraph e-mail, what can you do with all the communication tools at your disposal?

■ **MENTOR:**	*Taryn Rose*
■ **BUSINESS:**	*Taryn Rose International*
■ **LOCATION:**	*Los Angeles, California, U.S.A.*
■ **INDUSTRY:**	*Fashion Footwear*

ONE WOMAN WHO DID IT RIGHT

Like many other women, Taryn Rose has a thing for shoes. But unlike others, she turned this passion into a $20 million business.

Taryn got her start far from the fashion industry. She earned a medical degree from the University of Southern California and went on to become an orthopaedic surgeon. Although she loved fashionable heels, standing in them all day just wasn't working, so she spent hours searching for shoes that looked great but didn't kill her feet. The more she searched, the more she realized that such shoes just didn't exist. So, frustrated in her search and inspired by the daily surgeries she performed to correct damage caused by poorly fitting shoes, she made the decision to launch Taryn Rose International.

In 1998, shortly after obtaining a start-up loan and setting up business in her home, Taryn excitedly boxed up and shipped her first pair of shoes. And from that first pair on, Taryn's business and popularity have taken off.

From supplying the prestigious shoe department of Nordstrom to launching her own boutiques to national recognition by the U.S. Small Business Administration to placement of her shoes at the Oscars, Taryn understands the value of instilling confidence in others—and she's constantly doing just that.

HOW SHE DID IT

Taryn's decision to leave her medical practice to launch a shoe business met with serious family resistance. The daughter of Vietnamese refugees, Taryn always lived up to her parents' high standards of success. They were proud of her medical career and it seemed the "appropriate" path for her to travel the rest of her life. So they were stymied by her idea to design and sell shoes. Although it was difficult to go against their advice, Taryn made her decision—she knew her idea would succeed, and that she would always feel like a failure if she did not listen to her heart. Led by her strong will and passion, Taryn followed her heart.

As she built her business, Taryn relied on the innate ability she always had: the ability to inspire confidence in those around her. Taryn tracks this confidence back to her work as a surgeon, when she developed the ability to remain calm no matter what the circumstances. As she moved from medicine to the footwear business, she carried this confidence with her.

But beyond her medical background, Taryn's confidence arises from her custom of being fully prepared. When approaching a new concept, she researches it completely to be able to discuss the topic knowledgeably. Her willingness to invest the required time to really understand specific ideas has been a key to the success of Taryn Rose International.

Knowledge alone, however, does not equate success. It must be complemented by one very crucial trait: the ability to communicate. Taryn has mastered the art of communicating not only her *knowledge,* but her *vision* to her employees. She learned early on that sharing her knowledge, vision, and strategy would help her staff understand the "why" of their jobs, enabling them to achieve Taryn's individual goals for her employees, as well as the goals set for the organization as a whole.

From the outset, Taryn took a unique approach to staff building by focusing on individual employees. Because she started her business as a one-person shop, she understood every task and every employee's role. This helped her to be an understanding, hands-on manager, without micromanaging; and enabled her to attend to the needs of every employee, providing individual attention and supporting each one's personal and professional goals through training and outside classes.

Recognizing that compensation was a key driver of employee satisfaction, Taryn developed an innovative system of financial rewards. In addition to competitive salaries and benefits, Taryn puts 3 percent of the company's net profit into a profit "pot." Every employee, regardless of his or her position, receives an equal share of this profit "pot." And Taryn provides a separate across-the-board bonus when the company excels. Regardless of whether they are secretaries or managers, Taryn's employees trust that they will share in her success. Her innovative and egalitarian bonus system underscores the value she places on *every* employee in her company and her understanding that *each* individual impacts the bottom line. Taryn's reasoning for her unique reward system is simple: If *every* employee in *every* position performs well, the company will operate smoothly and she will retain great employees at *all* levels.

Because Taryn recognizes the value of every employee, they all feel confident about their roles in the organization. This confidence drives them to create quality products and maintain good relationships with customers and vendors. Taryn puts stock in her employees and they, in turn, put stock into Taryn Rose International.

WHAT SHE ACHIEVED

Just seven years into business, Taryn Rose finds herself atop a $20 million company. Her products are now in four of her own Taryn Rose boutiques across the country, as well as in such prestigious retail stores as Nordstrom, Neiman Marcus, and Saks Fifth Avenue. They can also be found on the Internet or ordered over the phone, making her products accessible to anyone in the world.

Taryn's unique vision has inspired her staff and her customers. She believes in her product and her optimism shines through in both her ideas and her merchandise. Taryn didn't start her company to make a quick buck. She had a dream of fashionable, comfortable footwear that could be worn by anyone for any occasion . . . and she made it happen.

For the past several years, Taryn has drawn on both her business and her personal expertise to support the community of women entrepreneurs. Becoming a member of the Women Presidents' Organization (WPO) gave her a chance to share her experiences with likeminded women. She finds that this collaboration generates more business for women, and gives them a chance to share ideas with others who might be experiencing the same ups and downs. Besides WPO, Taryn's success has allowed her to participate in and provide financial support to a variety of charitable organizations, which she does with gratitude.

Through savvy marketing, Taryn has caught the eye of the media. She's appeared on *CNN News, Good Morning America,* and the highly coveted *Oprah Winfrey Show,* in addition to regional shows across the country. Taryn and her products appear regularly in the fashion editorials of top magazines, and in 2005, *Fast Company* magazine named Taryn as #1 on its list of Top Women Business Builders of the year.

After transforming her idea into a thriving business, Taryn feels that her company is now truly positioned for growth. She believes there is no limit to where it can go. She recently launched her line of men's shoes and, after much persistence, managed to get Jamie Foxx to wear a pair to the Oscars. This media home run cracked the men's market wide open for her.

Taryn continues to inspire those around her to believe in her products and share the vision of Taryn Rose International. She has built a staff of dedicated employees, and her reward system continues to achieve its goals: retaining top employees while creating an exuberant and confident team.

Taryn made the jump from foot surgery to foot fashion because she saw a clear market need. She had a front-row seat to an overlooked universal problem and recognized that she was in the perfect position to solve it. Her expertise, creativity, and confidence enabled her to marry comfort and fashion to create a line of products that stand alone in the world of fashion footwear.

These days, Taryn's products sell themselves, but it was her confidence in herself, as well as her shoes, that made them a best seller.

Niche Your
Business for
Influence

Developing Your Niche

6

Here's one of the most counterintuitive facts of business: You will increase sales and profits by narrowing your market niche. Now this may seem hard to believe, but it's absolutely true. And I've got a story to prove it.

In 2001, I was part of an entrepreneurial executive team driving a technology business. Things had been great for us during the dotcom era, but we were beginning to sense that the bottom was dropping out of the market. Although our business wasn't a dotcom, we *were* a technology business and could feel the shudder going through our industry. But, fortunately, before our company went down the hopper, we were able to find a buyer.

After dusting off myself from that experience, I debated about what to do with the rest of my life. I knew what I *didn't* want to do. I didn't want to start another company with lots of employees and multiple facilities and ongoing headaches. So I decided to identify a problem that I could solve (helping small and midsize businesses attract Fortune 500 accounts) and set up a simple business to do this (working from my home office with a few part-time employees).

GIVE BIRTH TO YOUR NICHE

I originally set up my new business to work with all kinds of business owners, but noticed that women entrepreneurs were a neglected niche. The more I researched the size and growth of this segment, the more convinced I became that this was a huge, untapped opportunity.

Over the years I'd read business books and taken courses that advocated a tight market niche. In fact, I had actually *taught* courses where *I* preached this message. But discussing something is different from implementing it. And despite confidence in my research, the idea of lopping off 70 percent of my ongoing revenue was scary. However, I made the decision to tighten my niche to women entrepreneurs, and that decision allowed me to evolve from a generic sales and marketing consultant to a recognized expert in my field. On a single day, I made calls and "transferred" my clients who did not fit into my new niche to other consultants. I had to take a deep breath to do this, as I'd previously considered those "other consultants" as competitors. I was taking a leap of faith.

But the outcomes of that leap have totally revolutionized my business.

BENEFIT FROM YOUR NICHE

Here's what happened:

1. *I no longer worried about competition.* As I looked around, I saw that I was the only one proclaiming to "work exclusively with women-owned businesses to help them access Fortune 500 accounts." I did this by really understanding how diversity certification enhances women-owned businesses and how to capitalize on it. (You'll also understand this after reading Section Three of this book.) And I did this by networking like crazy in supplier diversity circles. Before long, I knew all the key women business owners and all the key supplier diversity executives on a first-name basis. I'm not talking about local businesses here; I'm talking about the top players from across the country and around the world.

2. *I became an expert in my field.* Oh, sure, I knew a lot about sales and marketing, before my leap. And I probably even referred to myself as an expert in that field. But you're really not an expert until the market calls you one. Over time, as I

focused my niche more and more, others began to recognize my expertise, and the media began to refer to me as an "expert in growing women-owned businesses."

3. *I spent less time and money on marketing and sales.* By focusing all my marketing and sales efforts on women entrepreneurs, I was able to go deeper into my market at less cost. I could attend just a few national conferences a year and meet 90 percent of my prospects. I could develop a single set of marketing materials that would talk to 90 percent of my prospects. I could develop a customized Web site that spoke specifically to my target audience.

4. *I made it easy for my prospects to find me quickly.* With a single focus, I was able to rebrand my company from the generic Cantando & Associates (which said absolutely nothing about what we did—were we an accounting firm, an import/export company, who knew?) to WomanBusinessOwner.com, which spoke directly to our prospects, calling them by name. By the way, the fact that this Web address was available sent me a clear message that I had discovered an untapped niche.

5. *I positioned my clients as my cheerleaders.* With a company named WomanBusinessOwner.com, I made the decision to use only pictures of real clients on all of my marketing materials. So I gathered these smiling faces and distributed them throughout my Web site, on my printed materials, and even included them in PowerPoint presentations for my speeches. My clients were delighted to e-mail me their photos and give me permission to use them. But what's even more important, when I launched my new Web site, I sent them an e-mail with a link to their picture and many of them sent it on to everyone they knew.

6. *I increased my referral rate by more than 50 percent.* My prospects and clients now understood exactly what I did—"I work exclusively with women-owned businesses to help them access Fortune 500 accounts."—versus my previously vague "sales and marketing consulting." As a result, they were able to recommend me when they met other women who wanted to break into Fortune 500 accounts.

7. *Most important, this niche turns me on!* I never need to set an alarm because I wake up brimming with excitement and ideas. I e-mail my clients at 3 AM because I can't wait until a "reasonable hour" to share my thoughts. My clients, suppliers, employees, and colleagues tell me that my passion inspires them. And I love the very thought of that.

LEARN FROM OTHER WOMEN ENTREPRENEURS

Here are two other examples of women who created great market niches.

I know a photographer who specializes in family vacation photos. Depending on the season, she travels to the beach or the mountains or even to Disney World. She posts her travel schedule on her Web site and her sessions fill up two months in advance. Because she focuses on "Capturing Your Family at Play," she is perceived as a specialist and charges a premium price. She's a single woman who loves to travel, so she's built a niche doing what she loves, with the audience she loves, in the locations she loves. You can't get much better than that.

Another woman owns a car dealership that focuses on first-time buyers. She offers special financing for those with short credit histories, driver training for new drivers, and support in gaining insurance for those who have never dealt with this. She markets to students graduating from both high school and college, and to their parents. And she's making a ton of money doing this.

DRILL DOWN EVEN FURTHER

As a result of my success in tightening my niche, I decided to bring it in another notch. Over the past two years, I've focused on larger women-owned businesses. I did this for two reasons: these businesses can more easily see the benefits of accessing Fortune 500 accounts, and the larger the business, the greater interest it attracts from Fortune 500 prospects.

So, if my experience is any measure, the more tightly I define my niche, the more I'm able to help my clients gain success.

Why would *you* do it any other way?

■ **MENTOR:**	*Marnie Walker*
■ **BUSINESS:**	*Student Express*
■ **LOCATION:**	*Toronto, Ontario, Canada*
■ **INDUSTRY:**	*Transportation*

ONE WOMAN WHO DID IT RIGHT

If she'd listened to everyone around her, Marnie Walker would have lived her life uneducated and disabled. Instead, she overcame an unsupportive father, the Canadian cultural confines of her time, and a life-threatening illness to follow her dream and create her own business. Marnie's dream turned into reality in 1989 when she launched Student Express, a business providing bus transportation for special needs and French-speaking students in Ontario, Canada.

Born and raised in a small town in Ontario, Marnie had a knack for business. Although her father was a successful entrepreneur, he believed that women were valuable only as wives, mothers, and possessions. He thought they were inherently stupid, and that educating them was a waste of time and money.

At 17, Marnie developed a life-threatening illness that affected her ability to walk. After enduring eight years of surgery and therapy, she regained her health and learned to walk again. During these years of struggle, she defied both her father and her illness, and became one of the first ten women to receive an MBA at York University.

Marnie's power to overcome obstacles was a key in her ability to build a multimillion-dollar school bus company. Despite her challenges, Marnie prevailed against the odds to create a new niche in the transportation industry.

HOW SHE DID IT

It all started when Marnie learned that the school boards were having difficulty transporting children with special needs. The existing school bus companies were organized to transport large groups of children, in large buses, to local schools. They were not geared to transport high-risk, special-needs students to regional schools.

But Marnie was confident that she could do this. Through her personal experience with illness, she knew that it was possible to transport these children with dignity by addressing their special needs. One-size-fits-all did not work in this niche.

Her research indicated that there was a significant customer need in this niche, that competitors were not adequately meeting those needs, that the niche could be profitable, and that it had the potential to grow and be somewhat insulated from budget cuts. But most important, Marnie *wanted* to do this because she felt it was important. And this was the genesis of her company.

The school bus industry in Ontario was in decline during the period of Student Express's remarkable growth. For example, the York Region School Board, where Student Express obtained its first contract, had 1,400 buses on the road in 1990; today, they have just over 800. During that same period Student Express grew from 8 buses to 250.

The reduction in the number of standard school buses was a result of reductions in government spending. School boards reduced transportation budgets two ways: by staggering the start time of schools so one bus could service multiple schools and by increasing the distance students walked to schools.

Student Express, by focusing on transportation for students with special needs, was immune to many of these cuts because most of its students could not walk to school. There was also less opportunity to use a bus for multiple schools for the time the special-needs student was on the bus was often at the one-hour maximum already. And as special-education programs expanded, the resulting transportation contracts were usually given to Student Express because of its expertise and reputation in the special-education niche. Thus, while other school bus companies were awarded fewer routes each year, Student Express received more.

Because she was starting a company with limited resources and no reputation in the market, Marnie knew that a niche strategy was critically important. By tightly defining her niche, she could concentrate her resources in a single area. Focusing on her niche allowed her to develop a core competence, differentiate herself from the competition, and develop her brand more quickly with fewer resources.

Marnie knew that once she had established this core competence and reputation, it would be difficult for competitors to effectively compete in her niche. To make her mark, Marnie initially focused all her resources on special transportation for the York Region District School Board.

As a result, Student Express's reputation for providing safe and caring transportation was established the first year. Then, in the second year, it was awarded additional transportation routes with York Region and obtained a contract from a new school board, the York Catholic District School Board. This was followed in the third year with a contract from the French First Language School Board. Marnie won these contracts based on referrals from her initial York Region contract. The reputation of Student Express enabled her to continually increase the size of existing contracts and win new contracts.

Marnie's business grew this way because she had targeted a niche that competitors chose not to service and one that was viewed as in-consequential. Strategically, this gave her time to develop her brand before attracting the attention and wrath of established competitors. Initially, the competition ignored Student Express, because it was small and serviced a segment of the market classified as difficult.

While starting out small, Marnie was careful to ensure that her niche was large enough or could be strategically expanded to allow economies of scale and become economically viable. Student Express initially transported only special-needs students to special-education programs. Over time, it expanded this niche to include all students attending special-education programs. This included students attending French first-language schools, religious schools, music programs, arts programs, and behavioral programs.

WHAT SHE ACHIEVED

Student Express became successful because Marnie went against the norms of an established industry. She succeeded in this niche market and met the unique transportation needs of these children because of the way she conducted business and because the operating model and organization of her company differed from existing school bus companies in the region.

Marnie's initial lack of industry experience actually turned out to be an asset. She had no existing infrastructure and no preconceived ideas of how the company *should* operate. This clean slate allowed her to create a customized organization to perfectly serve the needs of her niche.

In developing Student Express, Marnie implemented three key strategies that were unique to the school bus industry at that time:

1. *The name and logo reflected what the company did.* "Student Express" was easy to say and easy to remember. While competitors used the name of their founders or geographic locations, the Student Express logo on the side of each bus served as a rolling billboard. People saw Student Express everywhere and, in turn, remembered it.

2. *Overhead costs were minimized.* Marnie's competitors invested in large facilities with huge parking lots and bus depots. Drivers were required to travel to the depot to pick up and drop off their buses each day. In contrast, Student Express had a small office with a small amount of parking. Drivers parked their buses at or near their homes. Marnie initially outsourced all vehicle maintenance. These decisions reduced overhead facilities, as well as fuel and maintenance costs. This model also increased driver retention as drivers viewed taking their buses home as an advantage.

3. *Mobile Safety Supervisors replaced traditional office staff.* They rode the buses each day coaching drivers and helping to resolve problems. These supervisors developed close relationships with both the schools and the parents and were able to resolve little problems before they became big problems.

Marnie's novel approach to business, coupled with her willingness to continually reevaluate and make changes, became an instrumental part of the company's culture. Employees continuously searched for ways to do their jobs better; they were flexible and able to adjust quickly to changing market needs and customer demands.

In building Student Express, Marnie took a long-term approach. Her first priority was to build and maintain the Student Express reputation with initial customers. This reputation, and the references it produced, fueled all subsequent growth. Marnie's strategy always revolved around profitable business growth generated by long-term win-win relationships.

Marnie successfully sold Student Express in 2005 and is now focused on identifying an opportunity to start and build her next successful business. At the top of Marnie's criteria is to build a business that is interesting as well as important. She also must sense the demand for an unmet need and her research must indicate that the business will be profitable with potential for growth.

Attending business functions, trade shows, networking sessions, and seminars to search for her next niche opportunity allows Marnie to broaden her thought process. To stimulate thinking and spark creativity, she asks a lot of questions and listens attentively. Most important, she focuses on what people complain about. Such complaints reflect unmet needs and one of these complaints could be her next business.

Marnie feels that opportunity exists for women who are willing to take advantage of their natural intuition. She believes that by focusing your intuitive instincts and doing your homework, you can create an innovative niche that will differentiate you from your competitors. She's done it herself and she's ready to do it again.

Expanding Your Area of Influence

7

Are you one of the millions of women who dread selling? If so, you're about to learn how to sidestep the most distasteful aspects of this critical function. You're going to learn how to expand your influence. Now don't confuse this idea with traditional networking because it's much more deliberate. I'm talking about developing a strategic influence plan and then moving forward to make it happen.

CREATE YOUR TOP TEN LIST

Relationships are the key to business success, but because you can spend only so much time meeting and greeting people, you've got to be selective. So, the first step in developing your influence plan is to create your Top Ten List—a running list of the ten individuals you know who can make the most difference in your business. Then you should make a positive connection with each of them at least once a month. Now that doesn't mean that you simply send them your e-mail newsletter or new marketing brochure. That might have value for *you*, but you want to do something that will have value for *them*, and you want to do it every month.

What does a positive connection look like? Well, it could be sending articles that relate to their businesses or personal lives, or funny cards—something that says you know them as individuals. It could be a referral for new business, or a contact for a media interview, or an invitation to attend a luncheon or dinner meeting as your guest. This should not be a mass production effort where you send the same thing to all ten individuals. Rather, it should be a well-thought-out, personal engagement with each individual.

After you've created your Top Ten List, you should put a notice on your calendar to connect with each one each month. And then, every six months or so, stop and review your list with an eye toward individuals you've recently met. At that point, decide which individuals you should slide off your list to be replaced by more influential recent contacts. If you do this right, your list should become more and more impressive over time.

To expand your area of influence, you need to be visible and involved. You need to associate with influencers—with movers and shakers—and your Top Ten List is the place to start.

CREATE YOUR TOP 100 LIST

After you have your Top Ten List working, create a list of 100 key people who should know about you and your business. Working from this list, create a plan to connect with each individual once a month for a year. If you do this correctly, you'll find more value with these Top 100 relationships than you would with a database of 10,000 names. To be successful with this approach, you have to work it month in and month out, because if you haven't contacted someone within the past few months, then you are totally off his or her radar screen.

While these connections don't have to be so customized and time-consuming as those for your Top Ten List, be sure they are meaningful. You may see 6 of these individuals at a National Association of Women Business Owners meeting; then cross those 6 off that month's list. Maybe you sent Valentine's Day cards to 20 of them and copies of a relevant article to another 20, and so forth.

Even though each of these doesn't have to be an individual effort as with your Top Ten List, you can't just send your e-mail newsletter once a month and write off all 100 on your list. Because, again, your newsletter is about *you;* this interaction should be about *them.*

Once you've worked both your lists for a few months, you're positioned to move up the influence ladder.

MOVE UP THE INFLUENCE LADDER

Have you ever noticed how people tend to stay within a certain comfort zone of friends and business associates? They feel at ease relating to a certain echelon of individuals and they are out of their comfort zone in moving up the ladder. I'm not saying that this is necessarily a bad thing. I know some women who interact almost exclusively with the same business contacts they had ten years ago. But to grow your reputation dramatically, you've got to move up the influence ladder.

What do the rungs on this ladder look like? Well, depending on the needs of your business, they could be the spending power of the executives you're dealing with, the level of peers you meet with on a regular basis, the type of organizations to which you belong, or your role within those organizations. If you want to achieve serious business goals, you must step out of your current network and into a group with wider, deeper, more powerful connections.

But just how do you do that?

When I decided to become a nationally recognized expert in women-owned businesses, I knew that I could not achieve that goal by continuing to attend local chamber meetings. I had to move up the influence ladder from the local level to the regional, national, and then international level. This meant that I had to transition to organizations with more serious agendas, programs, and members. And I couldn't just *join* these organizations, I had to become a recognized player, because there's no reason to attend an event if people don't remember you were there. So I searched out the appropriate national groups, took a deep breath, and called the executive director or president of each group.

I told them I wanted to become involved and was willing to commit significant time and effort to their organization. Then I asked for their advice—not their "help" but their "advice"—on how I could best support their group. I then followed through on their recommendations—I did the real work that it took to be recognized as an important member of this group. And before long, I found myself sitting on international boards and national forums and committees. I was playing in the big leagues.

And the same thing worked for my writing and speaking. I started out writing pro bono articles for local, and then regional, newsletters and magazines. And although I still write for a few regional publications, I now produce columns for several national publications. Where I had formerly spoken at local women's meetings, I now set my sights on large regional, national, and international conferences. The key is to jump in and just get started, while continually seeking opportunities to move up the food chain and become a recognized expert in your industry.

How did I know when I had crossed the line? Well, there were a few indications. First, the media started referring to me as "the expert in women-owned businesses." *Enterprising Women* magazine asked me to write for it and invited me to join its Advisory Board. Then, I was asked to become a board member of the Women Presidents' Organization and to become an Ambassador for the Women's Business Enterprise National Council. Next, Women Entrepreneurs, Inc., asked me to become its "Growth Advisor" and write a regular column. And then I was invited to serve as an envoy of the U.S. State Department, speaking to international women about growing their businesses. And then, of course, I was asked to write this book for you!

As I move up my influence ladder, I continue to meet more influential women. And each of these women, in turn, positions me to meet even more influential women. Of course, I can't just sit back and assume leads will come to me—I've got to attend all the meetings, do all the pro bono work, and write all the articles that I've committed to. But without a doubt, this is the most effective sales and marketing approach I've ever found.

EXPAND YOUR INFLUENCE THROUGH PEER GROUPS

One of the most straightforward ways to expand your influence is by joining a peer group of other women entrepreneurs. In fact, most of the women profiled in this book belong to several of the top women's peer groups: The Women Presidents' Organization (WPO), the Committee of 200 (C200), or the National Association of Women Business Owners (NAWBO).

WPO

The WPO is a powerful network of 1,000 women entrepreneurs who own multimillion-dollar businesses and meet monthly in strategic cities across the United States and Canada. These meetings are highly confidential and their purpose is to discuss specific problems and opportunities with fellow members. Within WPO, we joke that our meetings are "not for sissies." By that, we mean that these are not "fluff" meetings and you shouldn't join WPO unless you're ready to discuss serious issues and make quantum leaps in your business. As an example of WPO's value, my chapter in Charlotte, North Carolina, has a member who flies in every month from Belize to attend our meetings.

If you meet the revenue requirement of $1 million for a service business or $2 million for a product business, there is no better investment you could make than joining WPO.

C200

Based in the United States with international members in Europe, Asia, and Latin America, C200 has almost 500 women members representing more than 80 industries. Entrepreneurs who qualify own and operate businesses of at least $15 million in annual revenue, so there are some heavy hitters in this group. C200 also has a very effective mentor-protégée program for women whose businesses are not quite to the $15 million level.

NAWBO

NAWBO has chapters in almost every metropolitan area of the United States and is allied with the World Association of Women Entrepreneurs. NAWBO provides opportunities for women-owned businesses of all sizes and industries to attend monthly networking and educational sessions.

Individual Peer Groups

But what if your business isn't large enough to qualify for WPO or C200? What if there is no NAWBO chapter in your area? Well, you should definitely aspire to join these groups, but while you're working your way up, consider developing a mastermind group of five or six women from noncompeting businesses who meet regularly to bounce ideas off one another. All of you should be in the same revenue range with about the same number of employees, for these qualifications will give you something in common.

While you won't receive the benefits of belonging to a powerful network, a mastermind group can be a factor in expanding your business. And meeting regularly with others who experience similar challenges can be one of the very best ways to grow your business and expand your area of influence.

■ MENTORS:	*Terry Neese and Barbara Kasoff*
■ BUSINESS:	*Woman Impacting Public Policy*
■ LOCATION:	*Oklahoma City, Oklahoma, and San Francisco, California, U.S.A.*
■ INDUSTRY:	*Public Policy*

PARTNERS WHO DID IT RIGHT

An earnest blonde with a Midwestern drawl, Terry Neese says she has a calling "to help more people start businesses and to help those who own businesses take them to the next level."

Terry, a well-known speaker, author, and media personality, has founded five companies, ranging from farming and ranching to staffing, real estate, and public policy strategy.

Born with Cherokee Nation roots, Terry has received three presidential appointments to the National Advisory Council on Indian Education. She's also received numerous awards, served on many advisory boards and councils, and was inducted into the National Women's Hall of Fame. And Terry was the first woman nominated by a major political party for lieutenant governor of Oklahoma.

Terry's energetic partner, Barbara Kasoff, shares her vision. Barbara is president and cofounder of GrassRoots Impact, Inc., a public policy strategies firm that connects corporate America and political leaders with small business owners, women-owned businesses, minorities, and businesswomen. Like Terry, Barbara's been a business owner for many years, and she's successfully sold three of her five companies. Barbara serves on the Board of Directors of the National Women Business Owners Council. She was a delegate to the White House Conference on Small Business and the 1995 recipient of the State of Michigan Women in Business Advocate of the Year Award.

In 2001, Terry and Barbara envisioned a single, combined voice that could speak for businesswomen and affect public policy on Capitol Hill. They achieved their goal when they founded Women Impacting Public Policy, Inc. (WIPP), a nonprofit, public policy advocacy organization for women in business.

Today, when WIPP has something to say, members of Congress pay attention. Why? Because the organization has created relationships with the movers and shakers, and represents the voice of half a million businesswomen. Here is the story of how Terry and Barbara expanded their influence.

HOW THEY DID IT

When Terry and Barbara founded WIPP, they began by contacting lots of people—not just the organizations that were advocating for businesswomen, but individual women entrepreneurs throughout the country.

They found themselves smack-dab in the middle of a massive communication and reeducation effort. Many businesswomen simply didn't "get it"—they didn't understand the value of political participation or the effect government has on business. Terry and Barbara told everyone, "If you run a business and are not involved in politics, politics will run your business." Their message was that drafting legislation is one thing. Fighting to change it once it's drafted is a whole lot harder.

Back in 2001, each of the existing women's organizations had its own agenda, and those agendas didn't necessarily match. Women business owners and businesswomen are a very diverse group. This diversity made it difficult for them to coalesce as a single group with clout, a group whose voice could be heard. So Terry and Barbara set out to find what issues these organizations had in common. Once they had a handle on that, they used those issues and the combined strength of all the women's organizations to tackle the Hill.

They had to reeducate senators and congressmen and let them know that businesswomen now had a single, clear voice. Mounting that type of educational effort is similar to running a political campaign. You have to start at the grassroots level.

The grassroots methods they used are the same ones you can use to expand your influence and take your business to the next level. Here's their advice on how to do it.

Get Involved in the Business and Political Community

Terry likes to say she's "older than dirt," so she knows just about every woman entrepreneur in the country. She believes the only way to get to know your peers is to network, get out there, beat the bushes, and meet people. Pick up your phone and call your peers. If you don't know people, introduce yourself. Join local, national, and international organizations. Attend seminars. Participate in Internet discussion groups.

Don't try to do everything on your own. Join forces and create partnerships with other women entrepreneurs in your industry. And don't be afraid of your competitors. Reach across the aisle and bid on large projects with them.

As a group, women have a powerful effect on every election, from local races to national ones. In the same vein, businesswomen can have a big effect on legislation that affects their businesses. The "guys" have played this game for years. They know the value of being plugged in politically. You don't build a million-dollar company without having your hand in the political pie.

Work Your PR Strategy

To influence public opinion and achieve your goals, you need to work your PR strategy. Think of it as a political campaign. Research the market, develop your plan, put out your message, and take it to people at the grassroots level. Create timely communications targeted to your audience. Inform and educate them. Reach out to customers, vendors, employees, retirees, business partners, suppliers, and others. Then mobilize this grassroots force to take action.

Here's an example: Through a membership survey, Terry and Barbara discovered that health care and the rising cost of health insurance were the most critical issues impacting women business owners. Their research showed that Association Health Plans would allow small businesses to pool resources to purchase insurance at more affordable rates. Armed with this information, WIPP made access to affordable health care one of their key issues.

But how do they get this message to the grass roots? By writing about it, speaking about it every chance they get, and encouraging people to e-mail or write their senators and send letters to the editors of newspapers. They provide sample letters on the WIPP Web site and use technology in creative ways. The trick is to make taking action—such as contacting a legislator—simple and easy. You can do this by providing your supporters with preworded e-mails, faxes, or letters. With today's technology, geographic boundaries mean nothing.

WHAT THEY ACHIEVED

Building a brand-new business model with WIPP, Terry and Barbara ventured into unknown territory—pioneers in spirit, pioneers in work, and pioneers in deed.

In its early days, WIPP's prospective coalition partners were cautious about joining in with other groups because of possible disagreement over issues and competition for members. Organizations will never agree on everything, but that doesn't mean they can't be partners. WIPP approached their coalition partners and said, "Let's work together on the things we do agree on."

Today, WIPP has more than 500,000 members and many coalition partners, including the Women Presidents' Organization, the National Association of Women Business Owners, and the National Association of Female Executives.

WIPP has given women entrepreneurs a seat at the table in Washington, D.C. On a regular basis, WIPP members testify before Congress and meet with White House leaders, including the president. Terry has met the president many times, providing input on a tax-cut legislation and health care plans for small businesses.

WIPP members have testified before nearly 150 Congressional committee hearings and participated in White House and Cabinet-level roundtable discussions and meetings on economic growth. And WIPP connected thousands of women business owners on the first nationwide conference calls with 2004 presidential candidates, including President George Bush, John Kerry, and Richard Gephardt.

On August 18, 2004, WIPP held 20 events across the country to celebrate entrepreneurial and electoral freedom. More than 1,500 businesswomen, congressional leaders, and other policy officials attended. Prominent leaders have been known to clear their busy schedules and make WIPP a priority.

WIPP hasn't achieved everything it's wanted to by any means, but that doesn't deter Terry and Barbara one bit. They achieved their major goal: WIPP is *the* voice of women in business in Washington, D.C.

Becoming "Famous" in Your Niche

8

Most of us can't imagine ourselves as celebrities. But it's kind of a fun idea, isn't it? What's the value of becoming a celebrity in your field of business? And how do you move in that direction?

As a woman entrepreneur, positive recognition is important to your business because it makes you interesting to clients and prospects, keeping you top of mind. And, once you begin to achieve this celebrity status, it takes on a life of its own. But this isn't all about your ego. There is a true dollar value to being the topic of positive conversation among those in your industry. You begin to sense the results when a prospect contacts you because she "heard you on the radio" or "read an article about you."

Follow along and you'll see how to develop personal brand recognition that will allow you to become "famous" in your niche.

DEVELOP YOUR SIGNATURE STYLE

Over the past few years, some of my clients have taken to wearing signature pieces of clothing or jewelry. One woman always wears a hat. Another pins an alligator on the shoulder of her jacket. Yet another wears a diamond-studded dollar sign on her lapel.

My personal signature is the color green, which represents Go . . . Growth . . . Money, My logo, Web site, and all my marketing materials are green; and I always wear green to trade shows, conventions, and speaking engagements. Every time I put my name or the name of my company out there, it's in green. Just look at the cover of this book!

Does a signature style make any of us more memorable or actually enhance our revenue? I don't have any hard research on this, but I believe it attracts attention and creates positive buzz, adding an element of interest and fun to you and your business.

And I think there *is* real value in that.

USE MEDIA TO BECOME FAMOUS

Publicity is one of the most overlooked business tools available. The goal in publicity is not to directly market your business, but to gain recognition and credibility as an expert in your field—in effect, to become famous. The media loves working with individuals who are very focused in a highly specialized field, and when you reach that point, they will spread the word about you and your business.

Use Your Web Site to Gain Media Interviews

If you've had any media exposure at all, be sure to list every bit of it on your Web site and include links to any articles you've written, as well as those written about you. To see what this might look like, go to my Web site, *http://www.WomanBusinessOwner.com*, and you will see a special section called "Press Room" that provides links to recent articles and interviews.

Another way to use your Web site to attract media is to add "spokesperson" and your area of business, such as "insurance" or "trade shows," to your Web site keywords. Because the media always want to work with experts, these few steps can set you apart and position you for frequent, high-status interviews.

Expand Your Visibility through Media Interviews

To benefit from interviews you need to develop consistent message points that work for print, as well as TV and radio. For example, I want people to connect me with *women who own multimillion-dollar businesses* because that concept is memorable, attracts attention, and paints a clear picture of my perfect client. So I always use that exact phrase. In interviews, when I'm asked to describe what I do, I say, "Well, Jane, I work exclusively with *women who own multi-*

million-dollar businesses. . . . " In pitching my first book, *Nine Lives,* I always said, "This book is about overcoming obstacles. It tells the stories of nine *women who own multimillion-dollar businesses. . . . "* It's important to continuously hammer home your message points. And I'm relentless about it.

Be sure to let the media know that you can serve as the local, regional, or national angle to a major event or a hot topic. For example, immediately before Martha Stewart was released from prison, I blitzed the media to remind them that I was the expert in *women who own multimillion-dollar businesses,* because, in fact, that describes Martha. As a result I was quoted in several regional publications and wrote an article on the topic for a national publication.

My Martha angle was a hit because reporters are always seeking unique, timely, controversial situations. In addition, they're always looking for extremes; that's why my *women who own multimillion-dollar businesses* is a hit, because these women are unique and everyone is interested in them.

Always treat reporters as though they were your best clients. I do my homework before interviews—I know what kind of stories the reporters write; I understand their deadlines; and I bring my key messages to weave into the discussion. And I follow up every interview with a handwritten thank-you note; I think these notes have been responsible for my high percentage of follow-up interviews, because almost no one today takes the time to send a personal thank-you.

BECOME FAMOUS BY WRITING ARTICLES

Besides having someone interview you, you can take the lead and write articles for industry and local publications. And you don't have to write them yourself; you can have a staff member or ghostwriter author them in your name. These articles allow you to present your expertise to a targeted audience without appearing blatantly promotional.

But how does a first-time writer find a publication that will accept her article? Here's how you can get your article published.

Propose a Winning Article

The shortest route to getting an article published is to ask your clients what they read. Now be reasonable, just because your clients say *The Wall Street Journal* does not mean that you'll get an article published in the *Journal*. But try to find out what trade publications and newsletters they read and review a few back issues.

Once you determine the patterns of these publications, send an inquiry letter or e-mail to the editor. By the way, you'll have much better luck referring to the editor by name, such as "Ms. Quackenbush," rather than "Editor." In your letter, state that you're writing to propose an article discussing XYZ. Then mention a few benefits your article will bring to their readers and include a short paragraph about your credentials. All this should be no more than one page. Even if you don't think of yourself as a writer, by following my process, newsletters, e-zines, and other publications will accept your idea.

Write a Winning Article

So what should you write about? Well, again, you can never go wrong if you start with your clients. Quiz them about their problems and then develop an article that addresses one or more of those problems. The article doesn't have to be long and complicated; it just needs to provide new approaches to solving a particular problem. Here's a quick three-step process that works for me:

1. Describe the problem and discuss the cost in added expense, lost productivity, shrinking revenue, etc.
2. Discuss how much easier and more profitable their business could be without the problem.
3. List a few ways to solve the problem. Describe how you've worked with clients to resolve it. And close your article by challenging the reader to overcome the problem.

When you start to write, write straight through and don't stop to edit. If you don't know where to start, get a tape recorder and just talk about the problem. Then develop your first draft by playing the tape back and transcribing your thoughts. After you've completed your draft, spend some time editing and fine-tuning. If grammar and punctuation are not your forte, hire an editor to proofread and correct your final draft. (Or, you can "cheat," as I do, by e-mailing it to a trusted friend for review; my daughter, Suzanne, always catches errors that I miss!)

And remember, you can always pay a ghostwriter to write the article and submit it under your name.

Develop a Great Title

Your title should be clear and easy to understand. Don't make the mistake of using clever phrases that people have to figure out. Keep it simple. I always mention a benefit in my titles, such as "Increase Your Revenue" or "Cut Payroll Costs." One of my recent article titles was "Simplify Your Marketing Message to Increase Your Revenue." This title is simple to understand and explains the benefit gained by reading the article.

CAPITALIZE ON YOUR INTERVIEWS AND ARTICLES

Besides the initial attention you gain from an interview or article, don't overlook the opportunity to extend the life of the publicity. Here are a few ways to do that.

Print your interviews and articles as glossy handouts. Now you have to be careful when doing this—you must get permission from the publisher and sometimes you'll have to get reprints through its printer. But this is well worth the cost. Whatever you do, never just photocopy an article. For one thing, that can be illegal, and for another, it just sends a message of "cheap." After all the effort to write and submit an article, spring for the few hundred dollars that it will cost to have your articles professionally reprinted.

Here's an example of the kind of handout you can create. A few years ago, I submitted an article to *Fast Company* magazine that became a runner-up for its annual *Fast 50* idea contest. Several of my clients from across the country wrote in to *Fast Company* to say, "Yes, Mary really does walk the talk. She has gotten my company into new Fortune accounts, etc." Realizing this would be a great marketing piece, I asked for and received written permission from *Fast Company* to reprint the article, including its logo. I then had a PDF designed with the article running down the center of the page and the glowing comments of my clients on both sides. I'm still using this piece today and you can see what it looks like on my Web site (WomanBusinessOwner.com).

Another approach is to send your article to everyone in your network. Remember your Top 100? Be sure to include them. I always send a short note saying something like, "Jane, I've recently written an article on how women entrepreneurs can gain a foothold in Fortune accounts. I thought you'd be interested in knowing about my approach. Please give it a read and let me know your thoughts."

By the way, I also do the same thing with press releases; besides sending them to the media, I send them to clients, prospects, and others in my network. I always try to include a short, clever introduction. For example, when I traveled to Tunisia on behalf of the U.S. State Department, I e-mailed the press release with the subject line: "Where in the World is Mary Cantando?"

USE PRESENTATIONS TO BECOME FAMOUS

You can convert articles you've written into presentations; and the flip side of this is true as well—you can convert presentations into articles. Of course, after you've created your presentation, you need to find a group to deliver it to, but this isn't as difficult as it might seem. I've developed a three-step process to gain presentation opportunities for my clients, and they're often swamped with offers.

1. Create a targeted list of speaking opportunities by researching organizations that your prospects belong to. If your business is local or regional, check the business calendar in your local paper or business journal. If your business is national or international, Google your target audience (for example, I would search *women entrepreneurs* and *women business owners)* to find appropriate organizations. Be sure to search for associations; for example, if you are a wholesale distributor of residential fire alarms, you might want to speak to the regional Association of Housing Contractors.

2. Put together a very professional package including a cover letter that reads, "I'd like to present on ABC topic to your

group at no cost; here are a few benefits that your group will receive from this presentation. . . ." Include a half-page outline of your talk and a half-page biography. If you've given any speeches or presentations for similar organizations, mention those.

3. Send these packages to your targeted list and follow up with a call.

Don't let the fact that you've never done this before deter you. As a professional speaker, I know that organizations are always looking for pro bono speakers who are experts in their fields. Jump in there and volunteer! Take presentation training or join Toastmasters International if you feel you need practice speaking before groups. Have something worthwhile to tell your audience and be prepared to offer them something specific. Sharing your expertise can really impact your business.

DON'T STOP UNTIL YOU BECOME FAMOUS

Positive recognition can springboard your business to the next level. So get out there. Develop a signature style. Position yourself for media interviews. Write articles. Give presentations. Become famous and watch your bottom line grow.

■ MENTOR:	*Rhona Silver*
■ BUSINESS:	*Rhona Silver's Huntington Townhouse*
■ LOCATION:	*Huntington Station, New York, U.S.A.*
■ INDUSTRY:	*Event Catering*

ONE WOMAN WHO DID IT RIGHT

Rhona Silver is the complete package: inspired entrepreneur, savvy opportunist, and committed humanitarian.

At the age of ten, Rhona began to develop her talent as a caterer, working in her family's business. From there, she went on to Lehman College and continued to Hofstra where she earned her law degree. So, beyond her outward style and charisma, Rhona is a highly educated woman whose legal and business expertise has propelled Huntington Townhouse to its status as the largest catering facility in the United States.

But Rhona never takes her #1 status in stride; she's always on the lookout for new opportunities. This talented woman, who lights up a room with her warmth and winning smile, has put in long hours from the day she opened her catering business. Then, in 1996, she made the decision to evolve her locally known business to national, and then international, renown. She decided to become "famous." Her first step was to purchase 20 acres that she believed would turn her business into a roaring success. She was right, and since then, Rhona has worked long and hard to develop her niche as an internationally recognized entrepreneur.

In her climb to fame and fortune, Rhona has garnered awards both within her industry as well as outside of it. She has served as a presidential envoy to the Baltic States and has been awarded the Ellis Island Medal of Honor for ongoing contributions to her country. She also puts great stock in her membership in the Committee of 200, where she interacts with other woman with the goal of advancing their businesses.

HOW SHE DID IT

Rhona is quick to tell you, "Just because my last name is Silver doesn't mean that I was born with a silver spoon in my mouth. But I do like to think of myself as the caterer with the *golden touch*." Growing up in the family business, it was only natural that Rhona would start her own catering business. But, to survive in this highly competitive arena, Rhona knew she would need to develop a special niche, so she decided to capitalize on her creativity and intuitive sense of design.

As she looked around her industry, Rhona discovered a real lack of creative display. By and large, she was competing against men who were just throwing chicken on a plate. By contrast, Rhona insisted on using fine china and other inventive presentation styles. Her attention to detail and focus on arrangement created a strong initial following and the beginning of her climb up the ladder of success.

To develop a reputation as a truly unique catering hall, Huntington Townhouse began to craft each event to the needs, culture, and distinct personalities of individual customers. As a result, Rhona developed relationships with her patrons that went above and beyond a typical caterer; for example, brides often came to her for advice in selecting their wedding gowns. Rhona felt that once someone became her client they became part of her family. That's how she took a failing business, the run-down Huntington Townhouse, and built a successful company—Rhona Silver's Huntington Townhouse.

As her Huntington Townhouse began to grow, word about Rhona's unique capabilities spread as far as Israel. And when Prime Minister Ariel Sharon visited the United States, Rhona catered an event for him. Once the Huntington Townhouse began to receive publicity about events such as this, Rhona's opportunity was at hand. She knew that if she went the extra mile, and gave a million percent of herself to her business, she could break her niche wide open. She could actually become famous in her field.

To capitalize on this situation, Rhona used every talent she had and she let her creative juices flow. She put a lot of thought into special occasions and the role that food played during these events. For Valentine's Day, she thought, why not do bouquets of *chocolate* roses or heart-shaped spinach soufflés to spice up the romantic holiday? And for Halloween she displayed finger platters, finger-shaped mashed potatoes with red dyed almonds for nails. Rhona discovered that people loved these unexpected touches and before long, this type of creative catering began to win Rhona award after award.

As business at the Huntington Townhouse started to heat up, Rhona positioned herself to land TV and magazine interviews that, in turn, took her business even higher. And before long, the Huntington Townhouse gained the reputation as *the* catering hall for those planning a front-page event.

Although Rhona attributes her success to a multitude of activities, people, and personal experiences, she has always lived by a few hard and fast rules:

A winner never quits and a quitter never wins. "If Susan B. Anthony had given up," Rhona asks, "where would women be today?" Certainly not in the voting booth, nor on the floor of the Senate nor on the bench of the Supreme Court. Keeping this in mind, Rhona sets her goals and never falters. She works toward them one day at a time and has earned every bit of her success.

Be willing to take a risk. In building her multimillion-dollar empire, Rhona took lots of risks. But she was aware of the external forces that might cause problems and she prepared for them. Rhona knows if she hadn't taken those risks, she'd still be running a small catering facility that no one had ever heard of.

It's the team that makes the business shine. Although the business philosophy and strategy of the Huntington Townhouse may originate with Rhona, she understands that every employee in every ballroom makes it happen. She knows that her business shines only as a reflection of her team.

WHAT SHE ACHIEVED

When she takes a step back to see how far she's come, Rhona smiles with pride. Over the years, she's worked with phenomenal people and created small miracles for the special events in their lives.

Rhona's prominence in the catering business has allowed her to play a significant role in her community, and she leads many charitable initiatives. One of her favorite charity events, Wednesday's Child, allows Rhona to support a regional children's organization while having a lot of fun and promoting her business. At this party for more than 1,000 foster children, Rhona's team sets up carnival-like stations, with games and raffles. And, of course, they serve fun foods like candy apples and cotton candy. Rhona believes contributions like this make a real difference in people's lives. And she's always looking for opportunities to lead the way.

Through her Huntington Townhouse, Rhona has served the rich, the famous, the locals, and those in need. She's used food to help some celebrate wonderful occasions and to help others overcome difficult and painful situations. People have come to know Rhona Silver's Huntington Townhouse as *the* catering hall for a special event because Rhona designed her business with an eye toward creating that specific realm. Rhona always imagined what she would like customers to say about the Huntington Townhouse and then she created events that would drive those comments.

So how did Rhona Silver do it? How did she become "famous" and create a landmark business? She always focused on being creative and being different. From there, Rhona developed a "vision" of her success—what it would look like, what people would say about her and her business, how people would feel when they arrived at the doorstep—and she created a plan to make that happen. And, finally, Rhona took her plan very seriously and moved toward her goal—her vision—day by day. As a result of hard work and following her vision, Rhona became the owner of the world's largest catering facility. Having built a successful domain, Rhona can now capitalize it. As she looks to the future she is planning an investment with a hotel and wellness center or spa. The property on which the Huntington Townhouse sits is vast, providing Rhona with the space to add to her catering hall, which currently accommodates up to 3,000 people. Adding on to the facility would increase business and create a more attractive option for trade shows and conventions. So Rhona is exploring creative avenues that would appeal to this market.

Rhona considers herself blessed to be in such a prominent position. She looks forward to the future and is grateful for the journey of trials and triumphs that has brought her this far. Rhona's ability to relate to customers, be creative, and think on her feet has made her famous and has put her Huntington Townhouse at the top of the catering industry.

Targeting New Clients in Your Niche

9

Targeting new clients is a key to growing your business. By focusing on a niche that shares a certain set of characteristics, you can spend your time, as well as your marketing and sales resources, most effectively.

PROFILE YOUR PERFECT CLIENT

A great way to define your niche is to analyze your ten best clients. Ask yourself which clients you can least afford to lose. Who are your most profitable clients? Which ones would you like to clone? Then use this information to build a profile of your perfect client.

Your profile should contain the demographics that are important to your business. These may include industry, company size, location, and type of business (Do they sell business-to-business—B2B—or directly to consumers?). As a consultant, I work with women from all industries and my clients are spread across the country; however, client revenue is an important demographic for me because I've learned that businesses under $1 million in annual revenue are not in a position to afford my consulting services, so I work only with businesses above that level. In addition, because I can increase the revenue of B2B companies most dramatically, that demographic is part of my client profile. So I focus on women-owned B2B companies with multimillion-dollar revenues.

In building your Perfect Client Profile, you should also consider psychographic issues such as values and beliefs, decision-making style, or responsiveness to change. I use a highly unusual qualification when targeting my new clients. Because I work only with clients I truly like, I've developed a litmus test that's a little out of the ordinary: I work only with clients I can hug. Yes, you read that right. Before I agree to work with a new client, I must feel comfortable and she must feel comfortable giving each other a hug every time we meet. I don't do handshakes with clients, only hugs. And these aren't token hugs, either. My clients and I really enjoy hugging each other, so that's a psychographic component of my client profile.

The final elements of your client profile should include how you met each client, what type of work you do for them, and how your company provides value beyond your product or service. Here we're talking about what each client values most about you and your firm—what keeps them from crossing the street to the competition.

Capturing these last categories of information is important for two reasons. Obviously, with this information you can focus on finding more clients like these. But, and this is an element that we often overlook, thinking about and documenting this information also enables you to consider how you might improve your relationship and expand your business with these top clients.

Developing your Perfect Client Profile focuses your efforts and prevents you from wasting time and money chasing marginal or unprofitable prospects.

DEVELOP PROSPECT LISTS

With your Perfect Client Profile in hand, you're ready to develop lists of prospects to target.

Again, look at your current clients. Do these relationships provide any advantages or disadvantages in working with other companies? For example, if Intel is a current client, could that be an advantage to accessing a company like Dell or Microsoft? In some instances your Intel relationship might be a springboard into another technology company and in some it might be a showstopper. And the same thing might apply to geographic areas. A prospect may want to do work only with a vendor who has other clients in that region. I refer to building a prospect list based on your current clients as a "prospect trail." Let me show you how it works.

CREATE A PROSPECT TRAIL

In my previous business, which developed technical documentation and computer-based training, IBM was our largest client. I was able to take advantage of that starting point to land Digital Equipment (now part of Hewlett-Packard). Because Digital would work only with vendors who had extensive experience in the computer industry, I played my IBM trump card in selling to them. After closing Digital, I opened our Boston office, which enabled me to land AT&T, who worked only with vendors who had a regional presence. With AT&T as our first telecom client, I approached other telecoms and we brought Nortel and then Nokia and then Alcatel into the fold.

Although I've tracked that entire prospect trail in a single paragraph, it certainly didn't happen overnight. It took about four years to navigate the trail from Digital to Alcatel. But each of these prospects became a multimillion-dollar client and propelled our growth. In fact, just as our initial contract with Digital allowed us to open our Boston office, the Nokia deal enabled us to launch our Dallas operation, while the Nortel contract allowed us to crack the international market by opening an office in New Brunswick, Canada.

How can you capitalize on your current clients to develop a prospect trail that can lead you to *your* next big account?

BUILD FOCUSED PROSPECT LISTS

Here are a few other ways to build your focused prospect lists:

- Identify an industry with a particular problem, such as new governmental regulations; if you can solve that problem, build a prospect list for that industry.

- Find a psychographic niche, such as a commitment to recycling or a dedication to women's rights, and build a list for organizations sharing that value.
- Identify an association for which your company can provide a value added offering, such as group discounts for printing, and work with them to give you a prospect list of their members.

RESEARCH PROSPECTIVE CLIENTS

Once you decide on a prospect trail, industry, psychographic niche, or association to focus on, name a point person in your organization to find out everything about that category and the companies that could become your prospects.

Then, as you build your list of individual prospects, obtain all the information you can on each organization. You might even want to establish client forums, user groups, or focus groups to gather specific information.

After gathering information on each organization, drill down even further to understand particular individuals within those organizations who could be your prospects.

Really usable research takes a lot of time, and of course you can't stop running your business to become a researcher. So either work on this a piece at a time, assign it to a staff member, or consider hiring a research firm to help you really understand your prospect. I've also had great results using college interns for marketing research projects like this.

GO AFTER THE PERFECT CLIENT

I'm always on a quest for the Perfect Client. I've got my eyes and ears open for opportunities in the marketplace. And I'm always strategizing to figure out what my prospects will buy, why they'll buy it, and how they'll buy it. I budget 50 percent of my marketing dollars to attend specific conferences, trade shows, and awards events because that's where my Perfect Client hangs out.

In my quest for the Perfect Client, I focus my time and energy on the most profitable prospects and those who are most likely to influence others. I work hard to gain the attention of these two groups and spend minimal time and effort on the rest.

■ **MENTOR:**	*Kay Unger*
■ **BUSINESS:**	*Kay Unger New York*
■ **LOCATION:**	*New York, New York, U.S.A.*
■ **INDUSTRY:**	*Fashion*

ONE WOMAN WHO DID IT RIGHT

Kay Unger has enjoyed the rewards of success and endured the trials of failure. As cofounder and design director of Kay Unger New York, she's built a multimillion-dollar fashion company with seven divisions and more on the horizon.

Growing up in Chicago, Kay was always interested in fashion. As a child she taught herself to sew and put scraps of material together to create her first doll dresses. In her pursuit of a fashion career, Kay studied painting in the Washington University Fine Arts Program where her exposure to the arts contributed to her flair for color and her ability to use striking combinations of patterns and fabrics. She later transferred to the fashion department of the prestigious Parsons School of Design, where she earned her bachelor's degree. Following graduation, she enjoyed her first taste of the fashion industry as an apprentice for Geoffrey Beene.

Kay credits her current success to having experienced dramatic failure. In 1972, she and two business partners founded St. Gillian Ltd., which grew to a $125 million company before it went bankrupt in 1994. Fifteen days after she closed her old firm, Kay was back in business in a new company, designing a new line, Kay Unger New York.

Kay's father, a successful businessman and role model, always told her, "You're never a true success until you've gone bankrupt—known the bottom—and then found your way back up."

She did that and more. While working as a designer, Kay managed to find time to get married and raise two children. And she's always tried to maintain a balance between her personal life and her business life because she feels one is nothing without the other.

Besides juggling her family and her business, she was also a founding member of the Committee of 200, was a director of the Boys and Girls Club of America, and is a member of the Women's Forum and Fashion Group International.

HOW SHE DID IT

In the late 1960s, after graduating from the Parsons School of Design, Kay was one of three design assistants to Geoffrey Beene, one of America's most respected designers. She shared this job with Issey Miyake, the now famous Japanese designer, and Michael Vollbracht, currently the head designer for Bill Blass.

Each morning at Geoffrey Beene a new dress would be rolled in on a mannequin and the three assistants would work all day with Mr. Beene on this garment. They would study its simplicity and try every trim to pick just the right detail to finish the garment perfectly. While spending hours working on these thousand-dollar garments, Kay began to think about designing her own line of clothing. She was confident that she could make garments as beautiful as these, but for much less money. So she set a goal to "cover the asses of the masses." Although this broad target market sounds uncreative, Kay could think of no greater honor than to see her designs worn and enjoyed by thousands of women. These women, those who could not afford thousand-dollar garments, would be her niche.

A year or so later, when she had the means to make a move, she decided to go for it. She took $25,000 and bought assorted fabrics from Liberty of London fabrics and had them shipped to her home. She had no idea why or what she was going do with them, but Kay had taken her first entrepreneurial leap.

Before beginning her new venture, Kay first researched what the buying public in her niche would look like ten years down the road. She approached *Glamour* magazine and asked it to share its research on the future of the buying public. She discovered that the first wave of baby boomers, referred to as "war babies," would be the largest consumers of her products. She had stumbled onto gold. Because she, herself, was a "war baby," she realized that her target market would be women just like her and most of the people she knew. She would be able to develop products for this niche because she knew how they thought and what they valued. This knowledge gave her the confidence to move ahead.

At that time, Kay was guided by other professionals who looked at her work and said, "You're a fabulous dress designer. Focus on dresses. There are so few designers who understand them." Kay considered their advice and realized that her target customers enjoyed wearing dresses. So that's what she did.

Kay's goal was to dress women to look as feminine as possible. She felt that as women came into the workforce it was important for them to dress like women not men. One of her fondest memories is of a client who thanked Kay for selling her an unusual pale yellow suit with lightly beaded cuffs. She closed a big deal while wearing that suit and was convinced that being a feminine woman in a room full of men clinched the deal for her.

Kay's strategy has always been to know her customers personally. Understanding their needs has always been her best tool, and she does 20 to 30 in-store appearances for Neiman Marcus, Bloomingdale's, Saks Fifth Avenue, and Nordstrom every year. Kay knows better than anyone how to dress a customer in what looks best for her, so she feels it's important to travel to these stores and personally teach their sales staff everything she knows.

But what Kay knows goes well beyond dresses. And her current successful business proves that.

WHAT SHE ACHIEVED

Kay Unger designs have been worn by thousands of women. Kay has dressed Hillary Clinton and Tipper Gore for the Clinton inaugurations; Oprah Winfrey for the cover of her magazine; and Katie Couric, Jane Hanson, and Janice Lieberman for *NBC News*. Charlize Theron is a big fan of Kay's pajama line, Kay J's. And *Desperate Housewives* Marcia Cross, Teri Hatcher, and Nicollette Sheridan wear Kay's clothes every week.

Kay continues to expand her product line based on customer requests. She now makes daytime dresses, suits, evening gowns, evening sportswear, casual sportswear, and Kay J's, which are sold exclusively in all original prints for Neiman Marcus.

She now has an exclusive license for 18 home products with Bed Bath & Beyond; Kay Unger bedding designs are available in its stores and through its Web site. And you will soon be able to buy Kay Unger dishes, glasswear, bath products, and many other items for the home.

Kay's newest passion has been working with another group of designers, Georgina Chapman and Keren Craig of Marchesa. She helped these two London designers produce their first collection of couture and ready-to-wear, and she'll continue to produce their upcoming lines. Kay takes advantage of opportunities like these because she loves to recognize the talent of others and help them realize their dreams.

No matter what opportunities come her way, Kay will continue to do what has brought her success. She will stay true to her customer, because at the end of the day, that's her true inspiration.

Presenting Your Business in an Innovative Way

10

Your prospects may have hundreds of options for purchasing the product or service you provide. How do you stand out from your competition? What do you offer that they don't? How can you present your business in an innovative way to gain their attention?

DEVELOP A WOW STATEMENT

What's your response when someone asks: "What do you do?" Do you tell them that you manufacture and sell widgets? Do you tell them you're a consultant? Do you notice the bored look when you say this?

I believe that one of the hallmarks of business success is the ability to present your company in a unique way. Over the years, I've developed an attention-getting approach that does just that. I call it a WOW statement and here's how it works.

When someone asks, "What do you do?" I respond by explaining the problem that my clients face and how I help them resolve that problem. So, the WOW statement for WomanBusinessOwner.com is: "I've noticed that women business owners struggle to find new customers. Well, I work exclusively with women who own multimillion-dollar businesses to help them gain new Fortune accounts."

You'll notice that I haven't commented on what I do or how I do it; I've focused entirely on the results my clients gain from working with me. When I make this statement, the response I most often hear is "WOW, how do you do that?" Or "WOW, I'd like to talk with you more about that." Or "WOW, I know someone who could use that." So that's why I call it a WOW statement.

Developing my WOW statement has really set me apart. And WOW statements I've developed with my clients have allowed them to present their businesses in unique ways as well.

What would your WOW statement sound like? What problem do your clients struggle with and what results do you bring to them?

HOLD A CLIENT APPRECIATION EVENT

Unless you run a destination business, such as a day spa, restaurant, or retail shop, open houses are generally a waste of time and money. Who really wants to visit a nondescript office after business hours to eat overpriced appetizers and drink inexpensive wine?

However, the second cousin of an open house—a client appreciation event—has worked wonders for me. Here's how I've hosted client appreciation events that attract qualified prospects.

Approach your clients about providing a client appreciation event in the form of a free seminar or workshop. You can host this for a single client and *its* customers at your client's site; or you can invite all your clients to your location, asking each to bring a guest.

Promise your clients that you won't pitch your services but that you will provide information of value to them and their customers. The goal is to make you look good by making your clients look good. The end result is a win-win-win; you give your client something, they give their customer something, and you get to demonstrate your expertise to their customers. If you do this correctly, at the end of the session, those in attendance should want to find out more about you and your business and should approach you about it.

MAKE THE MOST OF AWARDS

Almost every organization and publication sponsors competitions, but under the guise of false modesty, many women fail to participate. But once you understand the value of these competitions, you'll find you can benefit two ways. First, you can win these awards yourself and gain prestige, credibility, and visibility. Second, you can nominate your clients for these awards and gain their loyalty and goodwill.

Win Personal Awards

Being named the best of anything enhances your reputation and the visibility provides ongoing press and business opportunities.

But how do you get started?

The first step is to research awards sponsored by organizations you belong to and publications that you read.

Then decide on a particular award and treat your submission like a marketing campaign. Find out the requirements and deadlines for the application, schedule enough time to complete an A+ application, and be sure to submit it before the deadline.

Besides applying yourself, you can ask your vendors, employees, or even one of your clients to nominate you. How do you do this? You might phrase it this way, "Jane, could I ask you to do me a favor that would take very little time, but would mean a great deal to me? I've always wanted to win the ABC Award, and I think I'd have a good shot at it if *you* nominated me for it. I'd be glad to provide all the information to make it as simple as possible for you. This would really mean a lot to me. Do you think you could do this?"

Of course, Jane is going to nominate you. How could she not?

Win Project Awards

Over the years, I've been able to close big-name accounts by winning awards that recognized the innovation and quality of specific projects. What kind of competitions are out there and what kind of projects could win awards?

Start by searching for competitions through professional associations and regional organizations that you belong to. Focus on awards that will win attention from your clients and prospects.

The project that gained our company the most attention was a Web-enabled CD we delivered for IBM in nine languages. Back in the mid-1990s, this was a cutting-edge project and only two or three vendors in the whole world were capable of delivering this level of technology. We submitted this CD for an international award of the Society for Technical Communication, an organization of which I was a member. I don't think the judges really knew how to assess this project because it was so far ahead of its time. As a matter of fact, we submitted it under the category of "Other" because it didn't conform to any standard category. But by submitting something ahead of the curve, we called attention to our work and were able to win this prestigious international award.

Capitalize on Your Awards

Once you win an award, don't be afraid to brag about it. Besides the publicity that the presenting organization provides, you should create as much of a buzz as possible. Of course, you'll mention it in your marketing materials, list it on your Web site, include it in your newsletter, and send a press release to local and industry media. But here are some other ideas you might not have thought of:

- Host an event to celebrate. If your award is part of a group recognition, such as the Top 25 Women in Business, hold an event to recognize the other 24 women. The invitation might read, "Suzanne Smith, one of this year's Top 25 Women in Business, would like to honor the other winners of this year's award at a breakfast. . . . "
- Host an event for your company to recognize the part your clients and employees played in winning the award.
- Send a notice to your alumni magazine, either as a press release or an item for the news column. You might also pitch a story idea about how your university helped position you to win the award.
- Send a press release to the presenting organization, quoting yourself about the honor in receiving the award.
- Create a connection between the award and a current event or trend. Then pitch that idea for a media interview, mentioning the award as your credential for the interview.
- Include the award on your business stationery and business cards. Send these out with all of your award communications.

- Post information about the award, including the award logo, if possible, on your Web site.
- Edit all your bios and intros to mention the award.

And if you are nominated or a runner-up for a very prestigious award, even though you don't win the award, be sure to mention that as well. For example, in my bio I list that I was nominated as Office Depot's National Businesswoman of the Year and that I was a finalist for *Fast Company*'s Fast 50. My rule is: Even if I didn't win, if it's an impressive award, I mention it.

AWARD YOUR CLIENTS

One of the best ways to ensure loyalty is to nominate your clients for awards. Think about it. If someone considered you worthy to win an award and then went to the trouble of nominating you, would you consider them just another vendor? Here's how I've successfully won regional, national, and international awards for my clients.

First of all, I'm always on the lookout for appropriate awards. When I identify one, I contact the individual to tell her that I would like the honor of nominating her and I mention the benefit to her of the nomination. At this point, I sometimes hear, "Oh, I don't deserve that." Or "Oh, I don't see how I could win." Often this is just the false modesty that we've been conditioned to display. So I continue to pursue it and they almost always agree to allow me to nominate them.

To streamline my application process, I ask my client to provide me with all the information. I generally just e-mail the link or fax the form and ask her to send it back completed. Because she has all the information she can do a more complete job of this than I would, so I don't feel at all guilty asking her to do the real work. I then follow up as the deadline approaches to ensure that we don't miss it. Then when I receive her information, I complete the application and send it off. Often this requires no more than adding my contact information, which takes about two minutes total.

When my candidate wins, I host an event to honor her. Referring to my previous Top 25 Women example, I'd word the invitation,

"Please join Mary Cantando at a reception to honor Paula Perkins and the other Top 25 Women in Business. . . . " Hosting this event gives me the opportunity to get in front of the other 24 winners and allows me to create a special relationship with my client, Paula Perkins. How could another vendor pry Paula away from me after I've made her an award winner and then thrown a party to celebrate?

For even *more* ways to honor your clients through awards, see Chapter 20, where you can learn about our Woman Business Owner of the Year Award.

You can gain huge value from an award, but to really capitalize you must be sure the whole world knows about it! Combining awards with WOW statements, client appreciation events, and other innovative approaches will help you stand out and be perceived as unique in the eyes of your prospects and customers.

■ **MENTORS:**	*Leslie Grossman and Andrea March*
■ **BUSINESS:**	*Women's Leadership Exchange*
■ **LOCATION:**	*New York, New York, U.S.A.*
■ **INDUSTRY:**	*Conferences*

PARTNERS WHO DID IT RIGHT

When two social entrepreneurs collided at a financial seminar five years ago, the Women's Leadership Exchange (WLE) was born. These women, Leslie Grossman and Andrea March, are on a mission to support women entrepreneurs by sharing knowledge, resources, and contacts that uniquely fit their needs.

Leslie Grossman has been a successful entrepreneur and expert marketer for as long as she can remember. Besides that, she's a seasoned leader, having served as president of many organizations including NAWBO. Before cofounding WLE, Leslie was involved in research on marketing to wealthy women, a role that positioned her perfectly to focus on women business owners, many of whom are wealthy. Leslie was attending a financial seminar as part of her research when she ran into Andrea March.

Andrea March, WLE's other cofounder, was operating her seminar business, Investment Expo, when she met Leslie. After having run a multimillion-dollar jewelry business, Andrea had switched into the investment seminar field and found equal success. But after crossing paths with Leslie she knew an organization such as WLE could become wildly successful and could ultimately be her greatest achievement.

So these two highly successful entrepreneurs, with a joint goal of impacting the world by empowering women, founded WLE. In doing so, they've created an organization that functions primarily through regional conferences in major markets of the United States—New York, Dallas, Chicago, Southern California, and Atlanta.

To capitalize on the valuable time of their audiences, they've developed a rather unique format: a 12-hour, single-day conference. A WLE one-day conference presents powerful women who serve as keynote speakers, facilitates networking among the attendees, and provides women with valuable tools and knowledge to expand their businesses and their lives.

But beyond the conferences themselves, WLE's foundation rests on the personal and business commitment that Leslie and Andrea make to women entrepreneurs. And their efforts have not gone unnoticed. Besides constant kudos from conference attendees, they have garnered well-deserved media attention, including the prestigious Enterprising Women Advocacy Award from *Enterprising Women* magazine.

HOW THEY DID IT

Both Leslie and Andrea had always been committed to the needs of women. So their coming together just made sense. Shortly after meeting, they developed a joint vision to create more women leaders in the world, and they developed an innovative path to their goal. Through their unique experiences, they had each come to realize that money equals power. And the first step to creating this power for women was to create more money among women business owners. As the natural outgrowth of this line of thinking, they designed WLE conferences to empower and equip women with the tools they needed to grow their businesses.

Creating a unique structure for WLE meant sailing into uncharted waters. Leslie and Andrea had to develop an innovative way to appeal to the target audience. Because both women were actually members of their own target audience, it simplified the task. Both Leslie and Andrea had spent their careers supporting and communicating with businesswomen, so they understood the biggest problem these women faced was lack of time.

Leslie, who had served as president of NAWBO and joined just about every woman's organization out there, was familiar with trying to get women to "join the club." She was also familiar with the excuses women presented for not joining.

Andrea was also familiar with these excuses, but from the opposite perspective; she had evoked them time and again as a reason for not joining any of these organizations.

Their differences in this area helped them understand and accommodate both sides of their target market—the joiners and those who didn't join. If they could figure out how to combine these two groups, they could create an even larger target audience, with the potential of creating the largest network of women business owners possible.

While understanding the importance of networking, they also addressed the challenge that women faced in accomplishing this vital task—lack of time. Women weren't willing to invest their money, and especially their time, to attend just any conference or seminar. WLE had to provide something unique—something that no other conference offered to make women take the leap.

Leslie and Andrea knew one important characteristic of their seminars would be their "For Women Only" approach. Only women would attend and only women would serve as speakers. This would create an environment in which women would feel comfortable asking questions, while also providing the space for women to connect without feeling self-conscious. The dynamics of an all-women group would create a high energy level that Leslie and Andrea felt would produce an inspirational event.

WLE would also be unique in that the conference would move from city to city to provide the greatest convenience for attendees. Leslie and Andrea choose their locations strategically to accommodate the greatest number of women.

They also understood that the constant enemy—lack of time—would prevent women from attending a three-day conference, regardless of how close to home it was. So they developed a unique 12-hour-long, one-day event that would provide the same results as a three-day seminar.

After developing the distinctive structure of WLE, they added one more unique piece to the mix: star power. WLE would position women to interact with powerful, well-known female figures. Leslie and Andrea knew that this type of inspiration was exactly what women would need to gain the confidence to progress in their own businesses.

As they approached the launch of their first conference, Leslie and Andrea felt confident that their market was ready for this offering. They had done their homework and created a business that was unique from all competitors. Their "For Women Only," 12-hour-long, rotating-location conference with well-known figures was poised for success. They understood their audience intimately and had created a distinctive offering just for them.

WHAT THEY ACHIEVED

In four short years, WLE has attracted women running business up to $25 million and beyond. Leslie and Andrea have opened doors for women who might otherwise not have the opportunity to network. They have created situations in which women of all levels feel comfortable together and seek ways to help each other.

This occurs because WLE conferences empower women with the knowledge that they are not alone. At each conference, attendees see firsthand how important networking is to their success. WLE creates the network these women need by showing women business owners that there are *so* many more women out their just like them. And these women learn they can achieve more through partnerships with other women than they can by themselves. WLE works to empower women with this knowledge so they will use their networks to grow their businesses.

Although it's true that some successful businesses have small networks, WLE focuses on encouraging business growth by creating large networks. And WLE provides a network without requiring that women join an organization or club. Within a single day, women from different backgrounds, educational levels, and industries connect with others who can help them grow their businesses.

But some women are afraid of business growth. They are often running their families and their companies simultaneously, making time an even more valuable commodity. These women fear that business growth will mean more responsibility and less time. But WLE is working to change this misconception and help women understand that as their businesses grow, they will be in a position to afford great employees to shoulder some of the responsibility. As a result, they'll be positioned to take on even larger opportunities and add additional staff. The end result is an increase in personal time.

As cofounders, Leslie and Andrea understand what women need and they have successfully created an organization to provide that. They have established a community of inspired women who have been looking for a "place" like WLE. As it continues to grow, the WLE community attracts influential women who want to be part of their conferences and the WLE network.

But WLE's greatest success is in its ability to create an atmosphere of endless possibility. It is rare to bring together 700 women, each facing her own individual challenges, and have these women unite in spirit, passion, and drive. WLE conferences do just that— they provide the environment for magic to be sparked in every woman. Leslie and Andrea's innovation has created a truly unique outcome.

Certify Your

Business for

Leverage

Understanding Certification

11

Certification first caught my attention in the months following 9/11. I had just started working exclusively with women entrepreneurs to help them grow their businesses and, as I'm sure you remember, finding new customers in the fall of 2001 was tough going for just about everyone.

One of my clients worked in an industry that had been hit particularly hard. She had just been certified by the Women's Business Enterprise National Council (WBENC). Then, one day, out of the blue, a buyer from AT&T called to say that she had an upcoming project and was seeking a certified Women's Business Enterprise (WBE)—that's certification lingo for a woman-owned business. Long story short, my client closed a $28,000 sale with a single phone call that the *customer* initiated.

After witnessing this, I started investigating. I wanted to know what this WBE certification was all about.

LEARN THE NUMBERS BEHIND WBE CERTIFICATION

The concept of certification is really pretty basic. Certification proves that a woman-owned business is just that: The firm is owned and managed by a woman. As corporations become more and more interested in buying from WBEs, they want assurance that a firm is, indeed, woman-owned and operated, and not owned by a man who has put the company in his wife's or daughter's name. Certification immediately qualifies a WBE as a potential vendor with corporations who are seeking diverse suppliers. And the number of these corporations increases every day.

According to a recent survey by the Center for Women's Business Research:

- Almost 80 percent of corporations say they have policies to promote purchasing from WBEs.
- Nearly 40 percent of corporations say that all competed contracts require bids from at least one WBE.
- About 44 percent of WBEs say that certification was helpful in getting business with corporations.
- Some 56 percent of WBEs say that certification made a positive difference in finalizing a contract.
- Women who own businesses of at least $1 million in annual revenue are more than twice as likely to be certified as other women-owned businesses.

UNDERSTAND KEY CERTIFYING ORGANIZATIONS

WBENC is the largest third-party certifying organization in the United States. And WBENC certification is highly regarded by more than 600 major corporations, as well as many federal and government agencies. In addition to WBENC, a host of organizations across the country certify WBEs, so it is critical to understand if the corporations you are interested in require a specific certification.

RECOGNIZE WHY CORPORATE BUYERS
SEEK CERTIFIED WBEs

As I began to investigate corporate certification, I discovered that major corporations spend millions of dollars a year seeking WBE vendors. These corporations have entire departments to identify and solicit bids from certified WBEs. They spend millions in advertising and dedicate entire segments of their Web sites in the pursuit of WBEs. They also spend big dollars to belong to organizations, such as WBENC, that attract WBEs through events such as national procurement conferences.

Maria de Lourdes Sobrino, founder and CEO of Lulu's Dessert Corporation, knows firsthand the value of certification. She started her business 25 years ago, personally filling 300 cups with gelatin every day and packaging them for delivery to customers. But Maria has come a long way since then. Today, she counts Wal-Mart and Kroger among her national customers, and she has expanded Lulu's product line from single portions of ready-to-eat gelatin to 45 products and packages. Maria originally pursued certification at the request of Wal-Mart and every year Wal-Mart contacts her to verify that her WBE status is still current. When she first became certified, many of her customers didn't seem to care, but over the years, she's seen a definite increase in the requests for certification and the value it brings to her company. Several of her current customers now *require* that she be WBENC-certified to continue as a vendor.

KNOW WHAT DRIVES CORPORATE CERTIFICATION

Why are these organizations so concerned with finding WBE vendors? The reasons differ from corporation to corporation. In my quest to become an expert on the subject, I've met with hundreds of corporate executives who have titles such as Vice President, Supplier Diversity and Director of Diversity Purchasing. These conversations, coupled with other research conducted by my organization, have led me to group supplier diversity motives into four categories:

1. *Increased market share.* Many corporations recognize that women are the most significant purchasers of their products. Pharmaceutical, automotive, and consumer products corporations are just a few that fall into this category. In some instances, 90 percent of their products are purchased by women. These companies realize that WBE vendors help them attract women customers in a variety of ways. Using WBE vendors makes them aware of trends attracting women customers. Involving WBEs in product development, packaging, and advertising gives them insight into their key buyers. And, of course, they promote the fact that they make

significant purchases from WBEs as part of their public relations initiative.

2. *Contract requirements.* Many corporations encourage their
suppliers to include WBEs as second-tier suppliers, or subcontractors. And many organizations *require* WBE subcontractors for every contract over a specific amount, typically
$50,000. In addition, WBE subcontractors are often *required*
for government contracts. So these organizations use WBEs
as second-tier vendors to gain major corporate and government contracts.

3. *Process and product improvement.* It's no secret that women
have a different way of looking at things than men do. We
often question things that men take for granted, and we do
things differently. As a result, many corporations believe
that WBEs provide them with a competitive advantage.
These corporations believe that WBE vendors enhance process improvement and provide improved product design
and ideas.

4. *Regional growth.* Many corporations that are home-grown or
headquartered in a particular city want to work with local
WBEs to grow their local community. This is also true of
municipal governments.

Overall, these corporations use WBEs for hard business reasons,
and that's good news. They are looking at their bottom lines when
they contract with WBEs because we are their key customers, because we help win contract awards, and because we provide them
with a competitive advantage.

DETERMINE IF YOU'RE A GOOD CANDIDATE
FOR CORPORATE CERTIFICATION

Just because you own a business doesn't mean you should automatically jump on the certification bandwagon. However, if you fit
the following criteria, you should strongly consider applying for
certification:

- Your business is owned at least 51 percent by a woman or women, and managed on a day-to-day basis by a woman or women.
- You sell to businesses rather than individual consumers.
- You target Fortune accounts and can service them on a regional or national basis.
- Your revenue is at least $500,000; I've found that corporations seeking WBEs have a mind-set of "the bigger the better."
- You want to grow your business significantly, and can handle the growth.
- You have the resources and the cash flow to comfortably execute a contract with a minimum value of $100,000.
- You're willing to invest the time and money to complete the certification process, which typically takes about three months.
- You're willing to share your financials with the certifying committee. This includes the company's balance sheet, payroll, and income statement, as well as some of your personal financial information. I've found this requirement can be a deal breaker for some women, so understand that this is an absolute requirement before you invest any time or energy in certification.

If you fit these criteria, you should review the certification process that we'll discuss in the next chapter. If you complete this process and become certified, you'll be eligible to work with corporate buyers who are looking for WBEs.

UNDERSTAND GOVERNMENT CERTIFICATION

The U.S. government is the largest purchaser of goods and services in the world, and the average WBE federal procurement contract is $700,000. But rather than a single entity, the government consists of multiple agencies that operate independently of one another. And many of these agencies have their own certification process. So while it may be relatively simple to become certified by an individual agency, it's easy to get overwhelmed by the complexity of these agencies and the work it takes to actually get a contract with an individual agency.

Generally speaking, it is easier to gain government certification than corporate certification. But it's also important to understand that there are many *different* government certifications. For example, you might want to do work in your local community and to do this you might need to be certified by your city or county. This process is often as simple as going online, printing out, and signing a form that merely states, "My business is woman-owned." On the other hand, you might live in a community that has an extremely complicated process. The key is to determine which certification you need and then follow the directions to complete that process.

The easier it is to gain a particular certification, the less value that certification actually holds. So don't be surprised if after you complete a relatively simple process to be certified by your city or state, you notice that a lot of the businesses holding that certification aren't truly women-owned.

The most solid response you have to this "cheating" is to bite the bullet and complete the more complex process of gaining WBENC certification.

■ MENTOR:	*Mercedes LaPorta*
■ BUSINESS:	*Mercedes Electric Supply, Inc.*
■ LOCATION:	*Miami, Florida, U.S.A.*
■ INDUSTRY:	*Electric Supply*

ONE WOMAN WHO DID IT RIGHT

Like every good idea, Mercedes LaPorta's began with a light-bulb. Well, to be exact, it began with a $15,000 investment in Sylvania lightbulbs.

Born in Havana, Cuba, Mercedes and her family fled their homeland during the takeover by the Castro regime and ended up in the unlikely city of Chicago, Illinois. There she met and married her husband, Victor. After four years of battling the cold, windy Chicago winters, Mercedes was able to convince Victor to move to a climate more like the one of her childhood, and they ended up in Miami, Florida.

In 1979, Mercedes and Victor launched their business, then known as Mercedes Lighting, Inc., in a 1,000-square-foot office space. They sold a single product: Sylvania lamps.

Thirty years, and hundreds of products later, the company is now Mercedes Electric Supply, Inc., and boasts a 30,000-square-foot warehouse that houses more than $2 million in inventory, employs more than 40 people, and generates $25 million in annual sales.

From the single customer that she started with, Mercedes today supplies a wide range of electrical contractors, municipalities, schools, airports, and large hotel chains. And from her single product, she now stocks everything from wire, conduit, circuit breakers, switches, transformers, lighting fixtures, lamps, and ballasts, to programmable logic controllers, motor controllers, and variable frequency drives. And the list goes on and on.

Mercedes is proof of the power of combining a smart business idea with hard work and WBE certification. Starting her business with only $15,000, she's capitalized on her certification to turn a Sylvania lamp product line into a multimillion-dollar business.

HOW SHE DID IT

Mercedes's success, like any great accomplishment, was achieved by overcoming obstacles. Electrical distribution, like all segments of the construction industry, is heavily male-dominated. Getting her foot in the door of this man's world required tough work and lots of patience. She had to prove to everyone that Mercedes Electric Supply could provide the same, and in many cases *higher*, quality service as that of her male counterparts. And she had to do it at a competitive price. But, as Mercedes came to learn, certification can help women do all that—and more.

Mercedes first became certified by the government as a Disadvantaged Business back in the early 1980s. This certification allowed her to compete with other companies for contracts that had been set aside to support the growth of small local businesses. At that time, women weren't recognized as a minority and Mercedes didn't even become aware of such classifications until she discovered the

WBENC. Prior to that, Mercedes had been recognized as a Hispanic minority by the National Minority Supplier Development Council (NMSDC), but that organization doesn't recognize women as a minority.

As Mercedes learned about WBENC, she discovered that this organization was uniting women-owned businesses to gain national exposure, resulting in increased participation from both the government and corporate sectors. Mercedes learned that WBENC, as an unbiased third party, could ensure to government entities and corporations that a business they wished to purchase from was, in fact, woman-owned. Although Mercedes knew that the process to obtain certification required significant time and effort, she undertook it because she understood that WBENC certification would separate her—a true WBE—from male business owners hiding behind the facades of businesses placed in the names of their wives or daughters.

The fact that WBENC certification requires a significant level of documentation benefits large corporations and the government, as well as women-owned businesses, because it serves as a safeguard for both parties.

Over the years, Mercedes's certification has given her an incredible advantage over businesses that weren't certified. She earned her first certification with the School Board of Dade County, Florida. Based on this certification, Mercedes was able to land the Sylvania lamp contract for the entire Dade County school system. This $300,000 annual contract immediately demonstrated to her the value of certification.

Within three months of certification, Mercedes had a meeting with Office Depot, and within six months it placed its first order with her. Since then, her certification has opened doors to corporations from MGM Grand Hotels to American Airlines, where she was recently awarded a $10 million contract for the North Terminal at Miami International Airport. Mercedes recognizes that certification has been a key to her success, enabling her to unlock the doors to these major accounts.

WHAT SHE ACHIEVED

WBENC certification created an environment of opportunity for Mercedes. Besides exposure to major corporations and government groups committed to purchasing from WBEs, her certification has brought her in contact with remarkable women who have become her customers and helped her business in more ways than she can count. As a member of WBENC's National Women's Forum, Mercedes not only benefits from high-level networking, but she is able to give back to the organization and other women through her key roles on task forces and committees. Beyond that, she's also found that WBENC conferences and meetings are not only great for networking, but also as sources for developing friendships with inspiring women.

Beyond WBENC, Mercedes has also found real value as a member of the Women Presidents' Organization (WPO). And recently, when WBENC and WPO joined forces to bring together their collective members with high revenue into the Zenith Group, Mercedes accepted the invitation to join. Because major corporations seek WBEs who can meet their demands on a large scale, the Zenith Group has special appeal to them. Zenith members meet twice a year to share best practices of their businesses and to discuss and resolve current problems. And of high interest to Zenith members is the opportunity to meet with top Fortune decision makers to discuss upcoming requests for proposals (RFPs) and business opportunities on both national and global levels.

Today, Mercedes has a clear vision of taking her business to the next level. By 2010, she projects that Mercedes Electric Supply will generate $75 million in revenue. With the support of WBENC, WPO, and the Zenith Group, Mercedes is confident that she can achieve, and likely surpass, this goal.

But beyond her impressive numbers rests the fact that she was able to grow a successful business while raising two daughters and maintaining the strong family ties that are a hallmark of Latina women. Without her family, these business accomplishments would mean nothing to Mercedes. Her oldest daughter, Jennifer, who is currently working for her, will soon graduate and work for a fashion designer. And her youngest daughter, Katie, will finish college in two years. With these major changes in her personal life, Mercedes has more time to relax and enjoy a well-earned rest. But she is always looking for one more business idea. One more lightbulb.

Applying for Certification

12

Although corporations invest millions of dollars to search for certified Women's Business Enterprises (WBEs), an overwhelming number of women entrepreneurs have not certified their businesses. Many women tell me that they're overwhelmed with the certification process; they take one look at it and think, "Well, maybe next year." Although there's no doubt that certification by the Women's Business Enterprise National Council (WBENC) is complex, remember, that's part of its value. Because it's difficult to earn, it's virtually impossible to "cheat" the system. Therefore, corporations feel confident that if a business is WBENC certified, then it is, indeed, woman-owned.

COMPLETE THE CERTIFICATION PROCESS

Generally, the WBENC certification process takes three to six months depending on how efficient you are in completing your application. At any rate, it's a good bet that after you submit your application packet, it will take you at least two months to become certified. So the best thing you can do to shorten the process is to get started as soon as possible.

In the five years that I've been helping women grow their businesses, I've developed a streamlined ten-step process that makes your part of the certification less ominous. Here's my process:

1. Before you do anything else, be sure you qualify for certification. Here are the four basic requirements:
    - Your business must be owned at least 51 percent by a woman or women, and managed on a day-to-day basis by a woman or women.
    - You must demonstrate effective management of your business through documentation and established roles.
    - You must prove that a woman makes the company's strategic decisions by providing contracts, leases, and loans with your signature or that of other women.
    - You must prove U.S. citizenship or U.S. resident alien status.
2. Before you get started, check out the documentation requirements that are listed in the Checklist for Certification Documents in the Resource Guide of this book. This will give you a good sense of the information required.
3. Once you're confident that you meet all the requirements, and you feel comfortable providing the documentation required, you should assign a member of your staff as a certification manager. This individual will serve as the project manager in completing your application. Of course, you can serve as the certification manager yourself, but if you're not a detail-minded person, this isn't a good idea. Likely choices are your executive assistant, the human resources director, or the chief financial officer. You can also identify an outside consulting firm, such as WomanBusinessOwner.com, to manage this effort for your company.
4. Review the application at *http://www.wbenc.org/certification/ instructions.html*. Don't complete the application at this time but gather the required backup documentation in the following list, and then use that to complete the actual application.
5. Copy the Checklist for Certification Documents in the Resource Guide of this book and use it to gather all the required documentation. I suggest that my clients group their documentation in sections and assign a key individual to gather all the documentation for that section. I break this information into four sections:

- *General Information/Owner Eligibility.* You may manage this section yourself, assign it to your corporate secretary, or ask a trusted assistant to work on it.
- *Financial.* Your CFO or head of accounting is likely best to compile this section.
- *Management Information/Legal Structure.* This section consists of many historical documents. If you have a corporate secretary, assign it to that person; otherwise, you may want to involve the legal firm that helped you establish your legal structure.
- *Personnel.* The individual who heads up your human resources or payroll is the one likely to compile this section.

6. Group the documentation in the required order according to the Checklist for Certification Documents. I have my clients make two complete copies of this documentation set and put each one in a separate binder—one to send and one to keep as a reference.

7. Complete and submit the online application. After you have gathered *all* the required documents, use the information from those documents to complete the online application. Keep in mind that you can print out your application at any time. You can also open/update/close it as often as you like. But once you submit it, you can't make any changes so be sure you've got it right before submitting it. Once you're satisfied with the application, print out two copies (again, one to send and one to keep). Then, and only then, should you submit the online application.

8. Within a few days, you will receive an e-mail instructing you where to mail your application. Your complete application package should consist of:
   - Cover letter stating what is in the package
   - The printed application
   - Your documents, organized in a binder
   - The notarized, signed affidavit that you will be directed to provide
   - A nonrefundable check for the application fee, which is $300 to $350, depending on the WBENC affiliate processing your application

9. Wait. Over the next several weeks, your WBENC affiliate will process your application; this review requires some time because it is undertaken by a formal certification committee. When this process is complete, you will receive a call to schedule a site visit.

10. Prepare for your site visit. By definition, the site visit takes place at your place of business; it doesn't matter if you work in a downtown highrise or in a home office. A volunteer site visitor will come to your place of business to ask you a standard set of questions and verify items such as your signature on contracts.

UNDERSTAND THE WBENC SIDE OF THE PROCESS

When you submit your online application, your company and key information are automatically entered into WBENC's online database, and your certification status is listed as "Submitted" until your site visit and certification process are complete.

After your site visit, you should receive the news of your certification within a month. If your certification is approved, you will receive an electronic certificate and your status in WBENC's database will be upgraded to "Certified." You will then be automatically added to two Listservs: WEBuy, which provides sales opportunities for WBEs, and WBENC-Discuss, which provides information about programs and events.

AVOID THESE MISTAKES

I've talked with hundreds of women who've applied for WBENC certification and, without a doubt, these are the three areas in which most mistakes occur:

1. *Sending an incomplete package.* If you skip required questions or documentation, you can delay the whole process and lose a month or more of processing time. So double-check and then triple-check everything before you submit the application and send your package.

2. *Submitting the electronic application prior to gathering documentation.* The WBENC Web site clearly tells you that the clock starts ticking when you hit "submit" from the application Web site. If a major business issue pulls you or your certification manager away from gathering and submitting your documentation, you can miss your application deadline. Then you have to start all over again (sigh). So don't submit your online application until you have *all* your documentation in hand.

3. *Postponing the process of gaining certification.* I've heard horror stories from women who either miss out on big contracts or have existing contracts canceled because they failed to get their businesses certified in time. And don't think that you can pay an extra fee to "expedite" your certification; the process is fair, but lengthy, and there are few shortcuts. Get started now so that you'll have your certification when you need it.

APPLY FOR GOVERNMENT CERTIFICATION

After you gain your WBENC certification, you may decide to pursue government certification. But remember, there are as many types of government certification as there are government entities. If you're interested in bidding for government contracts, refer to the Resource Guide in the back of this book to learn how to take advantage of working with various governmental agencies. For further information about state, county, or municipal certification, check your state's Web site and search on "certification" or "minority certification." Or you can contact your state's business development agency.

CAPITALIZE ON THIS BONUS OPPORTUNITY FOR MINORITY WOMEN

If you are a minority, be sure to check into organizations that issue certification based on your ethnic status. A good place to start is the National Minority Supplier Development Council (NMSDC) at *http://www.NMSDC.org.*

I always advise my clients of color to apply for both WBENC and NMSDC certifications, and to do so simultaneously. These certifications require similar documentation and it is simpler to duplicate documents while you're working on one certification than it is to start all over again for the second one.

The good news for minority women is that corporations are especially interested in working with you if you're certified by both WBENC and NMSDC.

■ **MENTOR:**	*Carol Kuc*
■ **BUSINESS:**	*Complete Conference Coordinators, Inc.*
■ **LOCATION:**	*Chicago, Illinois, U.S.A.*
■ **INDUSTRY:**	*Conference and Meeting Planning*

ONE WOMAN WHO DID IT RIGHT

"Don't make money your goal. Instead, pursue the things you love doing, and do them so well that people can't take their eyes off you." It's not surprising that this Maya Angelou quote is one of Carol Kuc's favorites. Carol, who started her meeting planning firm 22 years ago, has captivated the eyes of many through her business as well as her leadership roles in organizations for women entrepreneurs.

As CEO and owner of Complete Conference Coordinators, Inc. (CCC), Carol provides national and international meeting management and registration services to corporate, association, and governmental clients. CCC identifies a meeting place, plans the logistics—food, beverages, hotel accommodations—and even manages the budget and financial requirements for each meeting. Carol, who is a Certified Meeting Professional, and her staff ensure that her clients' trade shows, conferences, and product launches are as successful as possible.

Her ability to see the big picture while paying attention to the details have allowed her to flourish in this business. Carol always seems to keep one eye on the major issues—providing simultaneous translators at international conferences, rescheduling venues following hurricanes, rerouting keynote speakers whose flights are canceled—while keeping the other eye on the minute details that add to that sense of perfection—fluffing pillows at corporate retreats, remembering first names, providing that special brand of candy that the client loves. Through it all, Carol balances her heavy load with a smile because every day she works in a business that she loves.

Beyond running her business, Carol is a well-known advocate for women entrepreneurs. She was a founding member of Women Impacting Public Policy (WIPP) and was recently elected as the president of the National Association of Women Business Owners (NAWBO). A presence in 33 countries, NAWBO supports millions of women entrepreneurs around the world. This well-known and highly regarded organization helps women grow their businesses by allowing them to share resources and knowledge with other women business owners from all walks of life.

It's no secret that, aside from CCC, Carol's passion is helping other women build and grow their businesses. By creating opportunities for women through her leadership in key organizations, Carol provides inspiration to women business owners across the globe.

HOW SHE DID IT

Before starting CCC, Carol worked as a court reporter. As part of her job, she was sometimes asked to organize meetings between the courts and attorneys to schedule depositions, hearings, and other events. As she planned and coordinated these meetings, Carol realized that she enjoyed this type of work and had a real knack for it. And she became excited when she realized there was a true need for this service in the business world. So, one day some 22 years ago, Carol held her breath and jumped. She left her job as a court reporter and started her own meeting planning business. From the first day, Carol knew she had found her true passion and decided to make it her life's work.

Then after 18 years in business, Carol decided to apply for certification as a WBE. Up to this point, the government had recognized CCC as a woman-owned business just through Carol's income tax filing and legal documents of incorporation. But Carol had discovered that corporate WBE recognition was different and had the potential to be much more valuable. As she delved into certification, Carol learned that corporations seek to achieve certain diversity goals. To meet these goals, they need to conduct business with women-owned businesses.

So, in 2000, she decided to apply for WBE certification to attract new clients and gain bigger corporate accounts. As she started the application, she realized that the process of *proving* her business qualified as a WBE was going to be a significant undertaking. Because she had been in business for 18 years, Carol had to back up and create a paper trail to track that her personal money had been responsible for the start-up and growth of CCC. This proved to be a difficult process. As a result, Carol advises women to develop a paper trail, which she calls a "follow-the-money" trail, as early as possible. Carol recommends starting your "follow-the-money" trail before you even open the business—as soon as the business idea pops into your head.

Proving the legitimacy of a woman-owned business—that a woman or women truly own and run it—is the essential key to becoming certified. A few years back, Carol had the opportunity to conduct site visits for WBE certification. Her job was to meet with WBE applicants to determine if their businesses had the proper paper trails to prove WBE legitimacy. As a result of this experience, Carol shares essential questions with women who are considering starting their own business:

- Who will own your stock? To qualify as a WBE, 51 percent of the shareholders must be women.
- Under whose name will the company be incorporated? Don't automatically include your husband's name unless he's an active investor or manager in the business.
- Who signs the checks and who owns the bank accounts funding your start-up? If possible, sign every check and make a copy for your records. Ensure that all the money leads back to your name.

Retracing 18 years of paperwork to prove CCC was legitimately woman-owned was a daunting task for Carol, but she was able to accomplish it with support from her administrative staff, as well as

NAWBO. Carol advises women seeking certification to identify resources to support their efforts rather than trying to do it all by themselves. It's essential to seek out organizations that can work with you or your staff in identifying and organizing your paperwork. She suggests contacting the Women's Business Development Centers. The centers, which are funded by the U.S. Small Business Administration, provide counseling on every level for women who either want to start a business or increase the size of their businesses.

Carol emphasizes again and again, the most basic, yet crucial thing is to keep a paper trail.

WHAT SHE ACHIEVED

Applying for WBE certification required a huge investment of Carol's time, but it was worth the effort. She recommends certification to any *serious* woman business owner because of the opportunities it presents and the doors it opens.

Part of the reason Carol was able to qualify for certification is because of her attention to detail and the fact that she had properly maintained her business records over the years. She advises other women, whether or not they have kept such meticulous records, to utilize their staff and outside advisors to bring together all the details that the certifiers are looking for and present them in an appropriate package. Having had the experience of backtracking, Carol knows firsthand that understanding the rules ahead of time and working with experienced advisors are two invaluable shortcuts.

After gaining her WBE status, Carol discovered that she was only halfway home. She realized that the next step to winning large corporate accounts was strategic marketing to capitalize on her certification. Her certification would prove to the corporations that she was, indeed, a woman-owned business, and that she was *serious* about her business. But to get that word out she had to announce to the world that she was certified. For Carol, this meant becoming more involved in organizations such as NAWBO. It also meant promoting her WBE status as a key selling point. Carol learned that as more individuals knew she was certified, the more her business would spread. So, using her certification as the foundation, Carol combined marketing and networking to create the potential for new corporate business.

Besides providing business growth, Carol's certification has led her to become more involved in helping other women business owners. She's learned that WBE status provides entry into a huge, already established network of businesses. And as she continues to move forward in *her* business, she always remembers to lend a hand to women who are just getting started. As proof of this, Carol recently accepted the national presidency of NAWBO so that she could leverage her ability to help as many women as possible. Because of the success she's achieved in life, she wants to help others succeed.

Moving forward, Carol plans to really capitalize on her certification. She intends to increase her marketing department and develop a new advertising campaign to get the word out that CCC is WBE certified. And she is also committed to continuing her leadership role in her own community, as well as in the global community of women business owners.

Because she attributes her ongoing success to certification, Carol hopes all women business owners will pursue it. Her success story is one of a woman who works hard and takes advantage of the opportunities of being a woman business owner. And she believes that any woman with a passion can do the same in whatever industry she chooses.

Making the
Most of Your Certification

13

If corporate America has awakened to the value of women as customers and vendors, why do so many women continue to struggle in marketing their goods and services to corporations? For every WBE success story, there seems to be a dozen women standing on the sidelines waiting for something to happen.

So what's the secret to capitalizing on WBE certification? As part of a complete marketing and sales plan, certification can be an effective way to make contacts and create shortcuts in building business. But certification is not an "if-you-build-it-they-will-come" solution. Like any worthwhile business endeavor, opportunities to capitalize on your certification hinge on your ability to research, plan, and execute.

RESEARCH THE CORPORATIONS

I'll give you the same advice I give my clients: Don't be greedy. Begin by selecting a *few* target companies that you want to work with rather than trying to tackle a hundred of them. For your first round, I suggest you select five companies to focus on.

Do your homework and research how each of these companies moves from identifying a customer need to delivering a final product or service to that customer. While you're investigating, find out what they are celebrating; understand their challenges; learn their jargon. The goal is to become a virtual insider with just these five companies.

After you've got a good understanding of a particular company's background, learn all you can about its organizational structure and supply chain. Almost every corporation has drastically restructured in recent years. The corporations have outsourced entire departments and collapsed levels of management, and they continue to look for ways to eliminate noncore segments. Look for the changes that have left holes you can fill. In some instances, those holes have been temporarily plugged; but there may be a way you can offer a more permanent or more cost-effective solution. Rather than thinking, How can we gain business with this company? you should be thinking, How can we contribute to the success of this company?

DIFFERENTIATE YOUR BUSINESS FROM THE COMPETITION

To contribute to a prospect's success, you must be able to articulate your value add. It's the purchasing officer's right to ask you, "How are you different?" It is your responsibility to respond without using worn-out phrases such as "customer service," "quality," or "lowest price." Those terms, and others like them, are not differentiators; they are the price of entry. Eliminate them from your vocabulary. How would you describe your business if you were prohibited from using terms like that? Real differentiators are items like shortened turnaround time, customized packaging, dedicated hotlines, or strategic alliances. Zingers like these will enable you to stand out from the competition to gain the business.

Valerie Shondel, CEO of Selecto Flash, the largest WBENC-certified screen printer in the United States, understands how to set her business apart from the competition. She provides customized catalogs for her larger customers and has developed a customized online ordering system that includes all the product illustrations, order capabilities, description, and pricing that her customers need to place an order. Valerie and her team have developed a valuable differentiator that puts Selecto Flash in a class by itself.

PLAN YOUR MARKETING APPROACH

Once you've completed your research and considered how you are different from the competition, it's time to develop a specific marketing strategy based on your WBE status. Here are the activities you'll want to consider at this point.

Create Marketing Collateral to Promote Your WBE Certification

To take advantage of your certification, you'll want to modify or create new marketing materials, such as brochures and flyers. Consider developing a separate marketing sheet to focus on your certification; this sheet should detail the customer's benefits of working with a WBENC-certified vendor. It's also important to develop marketing "messages" that you can work into letters, e-mails, faxes, and phone scripts. These messages can be as simple as one or two paragraphs that you carefully craft and have available to cut and paste into your messages with customers, prospects, and others.

Add WBE Content to Your Web Site

Decide how prominently you want to promote your WBE status on your Web site. It may be that you want to use your WBE status as your number one marketing approach. I know lots of women who've done this quite successfully; they proudly display their WBENC logo on their home pages. But depending on your industry, there may be situations where you will lose points by doing this. So analyze your situation, considering the pros and cons, before you make the change. At the least, you should create a separate page that discusses your WBE status and the value that brings to your clients. This page may be hidden on your site, but you can always send the link to interested parties.

Develop a WBE Marketing Calendar and Hit List

To capitalize on certification, you'll need to learn which diversity events have the greatest value and then track and attend these events. The best way to do this is by developing a marketing calendar that lists which events you'll attend, your goals for each event, your preparation and planned activities for each event, and your proposed follow-up.

Another critical activity is the creation of a Hit List. This may not be a politically correct term, but I think you know what I mean. This is your Top Five list from the research phase. This list should contain all the information you need to pursue these prospect companies and should define both your strategic value to them as well as how you will differentiate your business in selling to them.

EXECUTE YOUR PLAN

Once you've completed your research and planning, you're ready to move forward to make things happen.

Capitalize on Your Reference Clients

As part of your WBENC application you were required to list three reference clients. Of course, before you submitted these individuals as references, you contacted them and received their permission to do so. Well, here's the payout for that. When you receive your certification, you'll want to send thank-you letters to those individuals to let them know the good news about your WBE status. As you do that, research those organizations to determine if they have a supplier diversity initiative, and, if so, the name and title of the individual heading up this effort. Then send a copy of your letter to that individual along with your WBE-specific marketing materials and a handwritten note mentioning that you are a long-term vendor who recently received certification. Mention that you will follow up to ensure that he or she gains full credit for the dollar amount his or her organization purchases from (or spends with) your company. In WBE vernacular, this is referred to as "spend."

Then follow up your letter to supplier diversity with a call one week later. Try to schedule a meeting, again to ensure that he or she is gaining credit for the full spend with you, and also to talk with him or her about your offerings.

These individuals are generally happy to meet with you, because you're already on their approved vendor list. And here's the part that many WBEs don't get: To be successful in their jobs, these individuals must show that their organizations are working with diverse suppliers such as you. They typically demonstrate this by tracking their WBE spend, so you're doing them a favor by providing this information.

Promote Your Certification to Existing and Former Clients

After you've worked through this process with your reference clients, do exactly the same thing for all your existing clients. Send a WBE announcement letter to the client and also to its supplier diversity group. Remember, there is value to *them* in finding out that you are certified.

And here's one final version of this strategy. Consider notifying all your former customers and their supplier diversity groups of your recent certification. I've helped many of my clients rekindle the flame with old customers as a result of this approach.

Get on Every Database

Most companies with diversity programs have online profile forms that you must complete. When you contact a supplier diversity executive, the first question you will be asked is, "Have you completed our online form?" If the answer to this is no, he or she will direct you to go to the company's Web site to do this and then call him or her back. So save yourself this extra call by completing these online forms before you make your initial call.

These profile forms are located in various places on corporate Web sites. The fastest way to find one is to go to a particular site and enter "diversity" or "minority vendor" in the Web site search field.

Market and Follow Up

After completing your profile on a corporate Web site, allow one week before you call the diversity purchasing executive. During that call, you want to find out the contact information for the purchasing officer for your particular product or service.

Then call that individual and inquire about current opportunities for your product or service, as well as what you should do to be considered for future opportunities.

Your number one goal is to set up a face-to-face meeting with this individual. After scheduling this meeting, you'll follow the process that we'll discuss in Chapter 16, "Preparing for a Successful Sales Call."

GET TO IT

So there you have it. Research, plan, and execute. There's no magic wand, just hard work. But if you want to play the game rather than watching from the sidelines, this is the way to get in there.

■ **MENTOR:**	*Rebecca Boenigk*	
■ **BUSINESS:**	*Neutral Posture, Inc.*	
■ **LOCATION:**	*Bryan, Texas, U.S.A.*	
■ **INDUSTRY:**	*Ergonomic Chairs and Accessories*	

ONE WOMAN WHO DID IT RIGHT

She's been called "The Chair Lady," "The Queen of Ergonomic Seating," "The Texas Chair Diva," and other dramatic titles. But none of those is as gratifying to Rebecca Boenigk as her title of President and CEO of Neutral Posture, Inc., the first certified WBE to have been traded on the NASDAQ.

Rebecca and her mother, Jaye Congleton, founded Neutral Posture in 1989 after Rebecca's stint as a research assistant for her father, who was an icon of modern-day ergonomics. But it took Rebecca's own flair for business and outright tenacity to take the concept from a start-up company operating out of her garage to today's multimillion-dollar operation manufacturing and selling ergonomic office chairs and accessories.

Rebecca knew that her father's chair concept was a good product and filled a void in the marketplace. And although she and her mother knew very little about the competition in the furniture industry at the time, they believed they could make it happen.

Ergonomics was not a well-known concept in those days. Only the most forward-thinking corporate customers understood the risk-management benefits of purchasing ergonomic chairs for their employees. But Rebecca began educating clients using the most effective means available to her—a generous demo program.

"We basically operated on the same philosophy that good theater managers use," she laughs. "We had to put butts in seats!"

Rebecca realized early on that her chair made a good first impression on a customer's backside. "If you try it, you'll buy it" became her mantra. By selling comfort, value added, and personalized service, Rebecca was able to pick up some solid accounts such as UPS and Intel, which helped her gain a quick foothold in the market.

In addition to her customer savvy and ergonomic know-how, Rebecca used another personal asset to gain market share: her gender. As diversity became a buzzword in the world of government and business, Neutral Posture was—and remains—the only certified woman-owned seating manufacturer in the United States. Her Texas-based company now also manufactures in Canada.

With a long list of awards and honors, Rebecca is a sought-after speaker, board member, and advocate for WBEs nationwide. She currently serves on the Small Business Administration's Advisory Council and was recently presented with the Mary Lehman MacLachlan Entrepreneurial Excellence Award for 2005 by the Women Presidents' Organization.

HOW SHE DID IT

In 1996, one of Rebecca's corporate customers discovered that Neutral Posture was a woman-owned company and asked her to apply for WBENC certification. At the time, Rebecca didn't even know what that entailed. The certification process seemed daunting, and without her customer's insistence, she probably wouldn't have completed the application process. And once she received the certification, she filed it away and forgot about it. Rebecca did not yet understand the power of that piece of paper.

For the first two years following her certification, Rebecca didn't participate in any WBENC events. It wasn't until 1998, when UPS asked her to join WBENC's National Forum, that she got her first taste of what certification could do for her company.

While attending the WBENC Forum meeting, Rebecca met the supplier diversity manager for Texas Instruments (TI). She explained to him that she had been trying to get in the door with TI for five years but was always told that it was happy with its current supplier. Within three weeks, he'd arranged a meeting for her. Rebecca couldn't believe she was finally getting this opportunity.

Rebecca's meeting with the TI furniture commodity manager began with a lot of preconceived notions. She thought he had agreed to meet with her because his boss had made him. And he assumed that as a woman-owned business Neutral Posture obviously could not be "big enough" to handle TI's business. Rebecca dispelled that notion quickly. Once she got her foot in the door she had the chance to explain her capabilities and to show that her company was more than big enough and could provide better products, better pricing, and better customer service. Naturally, she closed the deal.

Since then, certification has played a much larger role in Neutral Posture's growth. As the understanding of supplier diversity continues to spread, government entities and corporations have been placing more emphasis on giving WBEs, such as Neutral Posture, the opportunity to compete. These WBE businesses still have to be equal or better in every category, but at least they now have a chance.

Over the past year or so, Neutral Posture's certification has helped more than ever. Rebecca has been receiving the kind of opportunities that she had never had before. But while competing for these opportunities, she keeps in mind that her certification only opens doors but never guarantees a contract. Even so, she believes many doors are opening for her these days because of her WBENC involvement over the past five years. During that time, Rebecca attended all of WBENC's quarterly meetings and most of its national events. She always shows up and gets involved. At these events, she focuses on developing relationships with the supplier diversity managers of Fortune 500 companies. And now *they* call *her* when an opportunity arises.

Looking at supplier diversity from the other side, Rebecca established a supplier diversity program for her own company. As a result, Neutral Posture is constantly working to increase its spending with women- and minority-owned vendors. Rebecca's purchasing department will not move to a new vendor without diligently trying to find a diverse supplier first because she feels that buying from these owners is the best support she can give to other women business owners.

WHAT SHE ACHIEVED

Because of the increasing emphasis on supplier diversity, Rebecca focuses her sales and marketing time and budgets in that area. Although she still meets with existing corporate clients whether or not they have a diversity program, her focus for new sales is almost entirely in the diversity area.

Rebecca used to joke about airline passengers who achieved Platinum status, swearing she would never "earn" that classification. But with the growth of her business, her travel has ramped up and she has achieved that status. And it all goes back to her WBENC certification. Rebecca is amazed at how busy she has become participating in supplier diversity events and meeting with customers who are seeking WBE vendors.

Rebecca has become such a well-known face at WBENC events that she has become known as "The Chair Lady." That's a distinction she loves because corporations remember what she does and now call *her* about opportunities for Neutral Posture. There is no call she enjoys more than that of a potential customer calling with an opportunity—to have them call *her* instead of the other way around.

Rebecca used to think that certification was just a pretty piece of paper, but over the past several years she has learned the true value it holds. She has also learned that a successful supplier diversity program begins at the top. Without CEO and top management buy-in, the program will not flourish and will serve as a major frustration for the manager and the diverse suppliers. When the CEO understands that this really is good for the bottom line, then the program will succeed.

As CEOs across the country understand that buying from certified businesses is not "charity" but rather the best bottom-line decision, their companies continue to develop or enhance their supplier diversity programs. Does it make sense for a corporation's vendors to resemble their customers? Of course it does. And this is what certification promotes.

As a seasoned CEO herself, Rebecca knows full well that WBENC certification will open doors but it does not provide a guarantee. And she's learned that there are many doors into every corporation. Sometimes she gets in through the front door and sometimes she has to try others. Supplier diversity managers serve as "door openers," and their job is to find viable and reputable diverse suppliers to introduce into the supply chain. Once the door is open, a woman business owner has the chance to compete. All Rebecca ever asks for is the opportunity to participate. Once she gets in, she can show that her products are better, more innovative, more available, better priced, and . . . you fill in the blank. What can you provide that your competitors cannot?

Developing Alliances to Capitalize on Certification

14

We all want to win. But winning requires a great team. In today's world of limited resources, the best way to create a great team is to develop alliances. Let's look at why and how you might build alliances to capitalize on your Women's Business Enterprise (WBE) certification.

RECOGNIZE THE TREND TOWARD ALLIANCES

One of the things driving business alliances these days is the concept of "bundling," or "strategic sourcing." These terms, sometimes used interchangeably, refer to the trend of combining multiple contracts into a single large contract. These approaches have become more and more popular as corporations and government entities discover that it is more efficient and cost-effective to outsource entire segments of their business. An alliance allows companies, who can't individually deliver the entire requirements of such a large effort, to partner with others to deliver the total contract.

This trend means that there are fewer opportunities to win individual contracts but more opportunities to develop alliances with other WBEs and larger corporations to win big deals. It is likely that you and potential alliance partners can bid more successfully on these strategic contracts together than any one can separately.

BENEFIT FROM ALLIANCES

Alliances can range from very informal, handshake agreements to extremely formal, large partnerships. Either way, they can be cost-effective ways to grow your business. Such agreements can help you deal with changing markets and technologies and allow you to side-step expensive, difficult, time-consuming changes to your business. Alliances allow you to provide credibility, bandwidth, and expertise in a certain area while avoiding the costs involved. Through an alliance you can break into a new market or provide a new service or product. And you can do that in a fraction of the time at a fraction of the cost and a fraction of the risk.

Alliances—done right—can make or save you significant money. And that's the baseline reason for all business decisions, right? But beyond dollar signs, alliances can strengthen relationships with key customers, help you reduce overhead costs, and allow you to focus on your core competency.

DEVELOP SUCCESSFUL ALLIANCES

The best alliances aren't about joining forces just to get bigger; the best alliances create a totally new solution that none of the partners are able to deliver on their own. The key to a successful alliance is to understand what value you bring to the other parties and what they bring to you.

I love what Marsha Firestone, president and founder of the Women Presidents' Organization (WPO), says about alliances: "A good alliance is one where you feel like a winner regardless of which side you're on. That should be your litmus test in any alliance, whether formal or informal. Everyone should feel like a winner."

FORM YOUR ALLIANCE

There are two ways you can become part of an alliance. You can wait for someone to approach you about joining or you can be proactive in seeking opportunities. A smart way to identify new opportunities is to ask your current clients, especially those who value your WBE certification, what additional services they'd like you to offer. You may even discuss the idea of an alliance and ask them if they can suggest potential partners they'd like you to team up with. By initiating an alliance on behalf of a client you can create a barrier to entry that will be tough for your competition to overcome.

Another approach to partnering is to check the Women's Business Enterprise National Council (WBENC) database for WBEs whose companies complement yours. They may be a good fit for partnering because they can provide one half of a solution while you provide the other, or they may service a geographic area where you need coverage.

Regardless of how your relationship develops, be sure you consult with your legal and financial advisors when forming your alliance.

MARKET YOUR ALLIANCE

Once you have developed your alliance, you'll want to market it to ensure that all your clients and prospects are aware of your joint capabilities.

Announce Your Alliance

The best way to announce your alliance is through a tiered approach. First, you'll want to distribute a press release. Besides sending this to the press, you should also send it to your database of existing clients and prospects and post it on your Web site. Also be sure to send it, along with a cover letter, to the diversity procurement executives of the organizations you're targeting.

You and your alliance partners should agree on the wording of this press release and each should commit to distributing it as widely as possible.

Develop Joint Materials

You'll also want to develop joint marketing materials that promote your unified capabilities. You might want to start by creating a joint logo to provide a separate identity for your alliance.

Next, you should consider joint brochures, presentations, and, perhaps, a Web site. If the time and costs to develop a joint Web site are prohibitive, each alliance member should develop a section on her existing Web site to promote the alliance.

GUARD AGAINST UNSUCCESSFUL ALLIANCES

So alliances are simple, right? Well, I wish that were always true. But we all know that problems can arise in any type of relationship.

I remember one particularly challenging situation I had with a Fortune company back in the early 1990s. Our technical services company had jumped through hoops to be designated as a "Business Partner" of this firm. As a part of our agreement, we were to help market its products and it was to help market our services.

Well, after we got into it, I realized that the tables were turned sharply in its favor. While I had dedicated my best salesperson to this effort, the partnering organization continually sent whoever was available at the time. As a result, my salesperson really understood our partner's products and goals, while we continually educated the revolving door of salespeople sent to support us. Over a two-year period, we sold a lot of its products, for which we made a small commission (not at all our goal in this partnership), and it sold absolutely zero of our services. When I finally put the numbers, including the opportunity cost of my salesperson, down on paper, I pulled the plug.

I learned two lessons from this partnering experience. First, before entering into any kind of alliance, make sure that all the parties will benefit fairly. And, once a part of such a relationship, if it feels wrong for any reason, and certainly if it doesn't make sense from a bottom-line perspective, create a plan to exit the relationship quickly.

INVESTIGATE GOVERNMENT CONTRACTING ALLIANCES

Let's face it, the government is BIG. And it works in BIG numbers. But as a woman entrepreneur, it's almost impossible to break in as a primary contractor on large government accounts. So alliances and, specifically, subcontracting, are great ways to start. Let's look at some specific programs the government has established to help WBEs get started as subcontractors.

Consider the Mentor-Protégée Program

One program you'll want to investigate is the Mentor-Protégée Program (MP) run by the Department of Defense (DoD). The MP provides incentives for major DoD prime contractors (mentors) to help women-owned businesses (protégées) develop technical and business capabilities. The purpose of this program is to prepare you to compete for contract awards.

Successful mentor-protégée alliances help create winning relationships for the protégée, the mentor, and the DoD. I've witnessed real success among protégées from various industries such as engineering, information technology (IT), manufacturing, telecommunications, and health care.

The best way to get started as a protégée is to identify a mentor at *http://www.acq.osd.mil/sadbu/mentor_protege/participate/index.htm.*

Learn about Government Opportunities

Many written resources are available to help women-owned businesses find and prepare for DoD contracting opportunities. The "Guide to DoD Contracting Opportunities" at *http://www.acq.osd.mil/sadbu/Doing_Business/index.htm* provides a wealth of advice for registering with and marketing to the DoD. This Web site also provides a list of Procurement Technical Assistance Centers that can help you develop a plan for working with the DoD. These centers, located in almost every state, provide training and counseling on marketing, financial, and contracting issues.

Check Out FedBizOpps

Because the DoD is responsible for 60 percent of all federal government purchasing, many WBEs set their sights on this organization. But if you're interested in working with other government entities, you should check out FedBizOpps (*http:// www.FedBizOpps.gov*), the single point of entry for all federal government procurement. This site posts information about all upcoming opportunities, and because contract awards to prime contractors are also published at FedBizOpps, you can use this site to identify subcontracting opportunities.

There are lots of government opportunities to consider, but let me offer some words of caution: If you want to approach these opportunities, you should do it full force. Working with the government isn't something you can do "on the side." To be successful in this area, someone on your staff must take this on as a full-time sales initiative.

MAKE GOOD DECISIONS ABOUT ALLIANCES

To develop a profitable alliance, you must identify the right opportunity with the right partner for the right reason. When making this decision, position yourself to do what you're best at and be sure that you feel comfortable with your partner. Above all else, be sure that your decision makes sense in the long run as well as in the short.

■ **MENTOR:**	*Ella Koscik*
■ **BUSINESS:**	*Management Decisions, Inc.*
■ **LOCATION:**	*Atlanta, Georgia, U.S.A.*
■ **INDUSTRY:**	*Consulting and Professional Services*

ONE WOMAN WHO DID IT RIGHT

Ella Koscik has taken a decidedly unique path toward business ownership. Armed with only her passion and business intuition, Ella left college early to take her first job selling secretarial staffing in Virginia. She soon discovered that she was a natural for this role. The staffing industry is all about people, and Ella's outgoing and energetic personality helped her quickly develop strong relationships with clients and coworkers alike.

Ella's success soon led her to Management Decisions, Inc. (MDI), at that time, a small IT staffing company in Atlanta, where she was offered 50 percent ownership of the company in lieu of a salary. After just 12 months, Ella quadrupled the company's bottom line and was able to purchase the remaining stock of the company.

Over the past 11 years, Ella has grown MDI to a $50 million national consulting and professional services firm with three divisions—IT Staffing, Medical Traveler Staffing, and Finance and Accounting Solutions. Her results have earned Ella multiple awards, but two are particularly important because they recognize MDI's long-term success—the 2005 Business Owner of the Year Award from the National Association of Women Business Owners (NAWBO) and the 2004 Built to Last Award from *Catalyst* magazine.

While Ella appreciates the recognition, she always explains that her driving motivation in building MDI has been to create a great place for great people to work. While it is always difficult for an entrepreneur to let go, Ella realizes that she alone cannot continue to grow MDI. Not only is she is always looking for the next great employee, but she also actively seeks alliances to capitalize on business opportunities.

Since becoming WBE certified in 2002, Ella has forged alliances with vendors, partners, and clients to capitalize on her certification.

HOW SHE DID IT

When MDI first received WBE certification, Ella had not yet begun to think strategically about how to leverage it. What she did think about was how to best meet the needs of her clients. So she did something radical. She asked her clients about those needs. Fortunately, MDI's clients included several Fortune 500 companies who were willing to share their perspective on certification. Then Ella did something radical again. She listened!

Ella's clients shared their frustration with the lack of diversity-owned firms that could meet their broad range of product and service requirements. They wanted to work with these firms, but were unable to find one that could, alone, meet their needs. Sometimes there were geographical constraints; sometimes there were prime contractors to work through; and sometimes the company wanted the diversity-owned firm to be the prime. Ella's approach was to position MDI as a leading certified WBE that could coordinate and consolidate all the resources that her clients needed.

To achieve this objective, Ella needed to form alliances. She began by leveraging MDI's certification and resources to identify vendors who could be a part of the total package that her clients needed. Next, she sought out partners by identifying large prime vendors who needed a diversity-owned partner as part of their larger contracts. And finally, she walked the talk by creating an internal Diversity Vendor Participation Plan to ensure that her company provided opportunities for other diversity-owned firms to supply products and services to MDI.

These alliances enabled MDI to show their clients the value of working with a certified WBE. Rather than just providing these clients with "diversity spend," MDI seeks to help them solve critical business and procurement issues.

Ella developed four key approaches to create diversity-related alliances.

First, Ella supported local and national diversity organizations. Ella has always believed that certification is just a piece of paper stating that you are a woman-owned business. Because you already know that you are a woman, where is its real value? Its value is that it helps you gain access to local and national contacts that can assist in developing your business. But *you* must get out and meet them by attending networking events at both the local and national levels. Beyond that, Ella has always felt that it is not just the responsibility of the business owner to be involved; both sales and management teams should be engaged with these organizations. It is through these organizations that you will identify potential alliance partners that will help grow your business.

Second, Ella sought opportunities in unique ways. She had always been aware that "Politics makes strange bedfellows," but she felt the same was true of business. She noticed that corporations were asking diversity-owned firms to work together to compete for larger contracts. So she was proactive about seeking out these opportunities. And she discovered them in unfamiliar places. Through MDI's membership in the National Association of Computer Consultant Businesses, Ella has been able to identify diversity partners who share the same commitment to ethical business principles. In several cases, MDI has established both prime and subvendor relationships with the same diversity-owned firms.

Third, Ella was always 100 percent honest about her organization. She understood MDI's strengths and weaknesses, and when seeking a partner, she focused on finding one that complemented her business. For example, because MDI was a service organization, Ella partnered with companies that could provide complementary products. She learned that corporations would respond favorably if she and her partners packaged an alliance as a complete solution.

Finally, Ella was proactive in using certified M/WBE vendors. Here she walked the talk. She realized that diversity-owned firms were constantly explaining the value of a diverse supplier base to corporate customers. And she understood that it worked both ways. By implementing a simple process to encourage and monitor use of diversity-owned suppliers, Ella was able to develop relationships with vendors to support her business, while also demonstrating to her corporate clients that she was committed to diversity. Also, because many of her clients were asking their vendors to report Tier 2 spend, Ella was able to use the program to support her clients' supplier diversity requirements.

WHAT SHE ACHIEVED

Since receiving her certification, Ella has generated an average of $15 million in annual revenue by participating in her clients' supplier diversity programs. This revenue continues to grow as corporations expand their programs and MDI develops the ability to deliver additional services.

Ella believes that diversity-owned firms must do business with other diversity-owned firms. To fulfill this belief, she created an internal Diversity Vendor Participation Plan, which helps corporations meet both Tier 1 and Tier 2 spend goals. This plan details how MDI identifies, manages, and mentors other diversity-owned suppliers while providing services to their clients.

Ella is proud of her Diversity Vendor Participation Plan. Since implementing this plan, about 25 percent of MDI's vendor spend has gone to diversity-owned suppliers. Included in this program are subvendors providing services to MDI clients, advertising and marketing firms, printing, office supplies, and many other commodities needed to run her business. In fact, seeking diversity-owned suppliers is now so ingrained in Ella's organization that it has become the *first* thought, rather than an *afterthought*, throughout the internal procurement process.

As part of this program, an alliance was formed with MSA Global Advisory Group. This alliance demonstrates the way Ella's entire organization thinks about expanding relationships. MDI's corporate vice president met the owner of MSA Global while attending a business fair to look for potential partners. As a result of that meeting, the two companies developed a formal partnership that has benefited both organizations.

Another alliance that was important for Ella to build included the leaders in the supplier diversity community. By gaining her certification and working with organizations such as WBENC and NAWBO, MDI connected with the women leading those efforts. Then, to further support the needs of their corporate clients, MDI initiated Supplier Diversity Executive Forums. These forums are attended by executives from both supplier diversity and procurement, and they are designed to help companies learn from each other while addressing critical issues in the supplier diversity community. As a result of Ella's proactive approach, MDI has earned a reputation as a thought leader in the supplier diversity community.

When Ella looks to the future, she sees corporations continuing to consolidate their vendor lists. She also sees corporations increasing their focus on supplier diversity. And she feels these two initiatives are not mutually exclusive. Ella believes that WBEs today must work together to build creative solutions to meet client needs. She thinks that corporations are waiting for, and will support, alliances of diversity-owned firms to compete nationally for larger contracts. And she is at the forefront, developing the relationships to create these alliances.

Throughout it all, Ella recognizes that alliances are not only about business. They are about people. The relationships MDI has fostered among diversity-owned firms are measured not only by the revenue they generate, but also by the opportunities they create for the people within those firms.

Making Things Happen at Diversity Events

15

Being in the right place at the right time can make all the difference in business. And supplier diversity events can be the perfect blend of the right people, in the right place, at the right time. While standard industry events typically showcase new technologies and products, supplier diversity events attract corporate and government entities looking for WBE suppliers.

All the major certifying organizations, including the Women's Business Enterprise National Council (WBENC) and the National Minority Supplier Development Council (NMSDC), as well as local, regional, and national government agencies, host supplier diversity events. You can identify the locations, dates, and times of upcoming events by researching each organization's Web site.

Think of a supplier diversity trade show as the mirror image of any other trade show you've attended. In a standard show, you arrange and pay for floor space, ship your booth, arrive early to set things up, and then stand in the same 10×10-foot space for hours on end. However, at a supplier diversity trade show, your prospects, the corporations and government entities, pay to rent the booth space and are responsible for setting up and staffing the booths. You play the role of "customer" by walking around, meeting with them, and discussing their potential needs for your product or services. As one of my clients put it, "It's like dying and going to Sales Heaven."

PLAN STRATEGICALLY

These events can be a powerful use of your resources, allowing you to gain face time with true decision makers. But you need to plan strategically to maximize your time. A typical procurement trade show lasts just one day, but I always arrive one day early and stay one day beyond the close. This enables me to plan meetings outside of the trade show to touch base with my clients and other WBEs to capitalize on opportunities that may come up during the event.

ARRANGE "MATCHMAKER" MEETINGS

Prearranged matchmaker sessions are a key component of most of these shows and many women I know have landed multimillion-dollar accounts as a result of a single half-hour matchmaker session. If you want to take advantage of these one-on-one presentations, you have to register early.

Details about matchmaker sessions are included in preregistration packages. To participate, check the show's Web site and submit an application listing the organizations with which you want to meet. You'll be notified prior to the event if you've been selected. Don't be discouraged if you're not matched up with every corporation you apply for, because there are always more applications than available sessions. Just focus on preparing for the sessions for which you're scheduled by visiting each company's Web site, researching its procurement program, and completing its online diversity vendor form.

If there's a particular company you really want to meet with, don't give up hope if you're not selected. Some women who are matched don't show up for their meetings and, if you hang out in the right place at the right time, you can often fill in for a no-show. The policy on substitutions varies from show to show; however, if subs are not permitted, that will be clearly stated on the matchmaker materials.

IDENTIFY YOUR TOP TEN LIST

Outside of matchmaking, opportunities exist to meet hundreds of companies at such an event. Rather than taking a shotgun approach, determine the organizations you want to focus on and create a Top Ten List.

When creating this list, think about the companies that you can best serve. Your list shouldn't necessarily be the biggest players but rather those you believe would be the best prospects based on your offering and geographic coverage. After you've completed your Top Ten List, use it as your game plan, allocating enough time to approach each of these prospects individually.

MEET THE RIGHT PEOPLE

Make it a priority to find out who will be on-site representing the companies you want to approach. Then call ahead to request a specific meeting time with these individuals.

Rather than leaving it up to chance, a preset appointment will help you stand out. It isn't always possible to arrange for this, but you can try. Whether you've got a formally scheduled matchmaker meeting, a "stop by to see me on the trade show floor" meeting, or you just happen to sit next to someone at lunch, you'll want to focus on the synergy between what she needs and what you offer.

I always advise my clients to visit the booths of the companies they're already doing business with. This is particularly important if the supplier diversity executives don't know you and aren't aware that their company is already doing business with you. Introduce yourself and ask how the business you're currently doing with their company can help them meet their annual diversity goals. Why should you do this? For one thing, it's a great conversation starter: "Jane, I wanted to meet you, because I don't think you're aware that I'm already a vendor for your metal products division." But even more important, by positioning "Jane" to gain credit for your spend, you're doing her a favor, and she's much more likely to help you in return.

LEVERAGE YOUR PERSONAL CONTACTS

We all know that personal introductions are more powerful than cold approaches. Think about which colleagues might have relationships with a particular organization you're courting and ask them to make a connection. But remember, this is a two-way street; you should also go out of your way to introduce other women to contacts that will help them.

Prior to the conference, touch base with women you know who are doing business with exhibiting companies. Ask them if they'll mention you and your company to their contacts, noting that you'll be attending the conference. Then when you introduce yourself, refer to your friend: "Jane Smith, of ABC Company, told me about you and I wanted to stop by to say hello."

GET READY TO GO

On the day of the event, be on the exhibit floor when it opens. Use the diagram from your registration package to map out a route that will maximize your time. Be sure to visit your Top Ten List and allocate enough time for browsing and engaging in conversations. Always dress in business attire. You don't necessarily need to wear a navy blue suit and look like you just stepped in from Wall Street, but you do need to look professional. Wear a comfortable yet savvy suit and ALWAYS wear comfortable shoes!

A reasonable goal for a one-day event is to have five key people remember you and your business. Besides the trade show floor, workshops, clinics, luncheons, keynotes, and receptions are all potential connection points. When you attend these networking functions, don't make the mistake of sitting with those you already know; I know that's often the more comfortable alternative. But go out of your way to sit next to someone you want to meet and really make an impression on that person. You want people to *remember* you!

GET THE INFORMATION YOU NEED

Your best bet at these events is to arrive energized and then move into your plan of action. Although thousands of people may be there, focus on the handful of quality connections that will most benefit your business.

While members of a corporation's supplier diversity group will be at each booth, it's not likely that the actual decision maker and purchasing agent for your product or service will be there. Be sure to get the supplier diversity executive's name and contact information, and while you're talking with her, ask for a business card. Jot down a few words on her card that will jar your memory back at the office. Give her one of your business cards with a concise handwritten message on the back that will serve as a reminder of how you can help her. Before you close the conversation, find out who is directly responsible for the purchasing decisions of your product or service and request that contact information. Before you walk away, know what specific information you will send to each person.

DO BRING THIS . . . DON'T BRING THAT

As with any business event, take along plenty of business cards. (And, for heaven's sake, if any of your information has changed, get new cards printed. Nothing shouts "unprofessional" more than scratching out and rewriting information on a card.) It's also a good idea to carry along your own tote bag to collect literature. Although you'll usually receive a corporate-sponsored bag when you register, these tend to be cumbersome and garish, and I like to carry something more professional.

A lot of women cart too much "stuff" to these events. Don't bring more than five sets of marketing collateral, each with a copy of the certification that corresponds to the particular event (for example, a WBENC certificate for a WBENC conference or State of Maryland certificate for an event sponsored by the State of Maryland). Understand that exhibitors will meet hundreds of women, each of whom wants to hand over a folder of marketing materials. Common sense tells us that most of these folders won't ever make it back to their offices. Without exception, supplier diversity executives I surveyed prefer you mail material to them after the conference.

FOLLOW-UP

Follow-up is easier if you keep things under control as you go along. When you return to your hotel room, review the cards you collected, summarize your notes, throw out any unnecessary items, and enter your new contacts into your database. But be prepared for overload. During my first show, I collected more than 300 business cards, each with a note on the back. Because I ran out of steam in the hotel room, I spent the entire four-hour return flight entering the cards into my contact database.

After each show, send a sincere, personal note to five important new contacts. I never think of these as "business" follow-ups but as notes to future friends. Although I always bring stationery and stamps with me, I often browse gift shops at the departing airport to find note cards that represent the area, and sometimes have these five notes written before takeoff.

When you get back to your office, be prompt in mailing promised material. If you're short on time, it's better to delegate this task than to delay in getting it out. Then continue the communication by picking up the phone. After all the effort you've invested, don't drop the ball in follow-up.

■ MENTOR:	*Katherine Henson*
■ BUSINESS:	*Avail Workforce Management Solutions*
■ LOCATION:	*Atlanta, Georgia, U.S.A.*
■ INDUSTRY:	*Staffing*

ONE WOMAN WHO DID IT RIGHT

What are you going to do when the company you work for gets acquired and, through no fault of yours, your job goes up in smoke? Cry and moan to your friends? Look for whatever work you can get? Or go out and start a business that resonates on a personal level for you and—even more important—satisfies a real need in the marketplace? In 1993, when her job disappeared, Katherine Henson chose "Choice C"—and never looked back.

Katherine's leap of faith was backed not only with inspiration but knowledge. As she often tells people, bad things often happen for good reasons. Before she could talk herself out of it, Katherine borrowed a modest sum of money from a friend and founded Avail Workforce Management Solutions.

Up to that point, Katherine had learned her craft and gained industry expertise through management roles with well-established temporary staffing companies. At TempForce, where she served as Regional Manager, Katherine transformed the company's operational systems. By the time TempForce was acquired by Randstad, Katherine's division generated an astonishing 40 percent of gross sales.

But she learned all of that was behind her, and she picked herself up and started a new business and a new life. Katherine started Avail with a grand total of one employee: herself. Today, the Atlanta-based company has seven offices and more than 1,400 employees.

From the beginning, Avail experienced remarkable growth, and, amazingly, that pace shows no sign of slowing. In 2005, just 13 years after she launched her company, Katherine achieved just under $100 million in annual sales.

But Katherine judges her true value in the difference she makes rather than the revenue she generates. She has used her new visibility and clout in the industry to advocate for workforce reform and improve the situation throughout corporate America for all working people.

Proud of her status as a woman business owner and her heritage as a Native American, Katherine is actively engaged with the Native American Business Alliance, Women's Business Enterprise National Council (WBENC), and the Women Presidents' Organization (WPO). She is a member of the prestigious Zenith Group, which brings together WPO members who are WBE certified and generate more than $50 million in annual revenue. Katherine is also involved with numerous charitable organizations that help women and children in need, and is especially active in helping minority women and men climb the ladder of success in today's workplace.

HOW SHE DID IT

Katherine's achievements, as a woman, as a Native American, and as an individual raised in humble circumstances, carry increased significance on several levels. Avail's astounding success is a direct reflection of Katherine's innovative and resolute spirit, her innate intelligence and charm, and her genuine people skills.

She capitalizes on her background and her strengths in a variety of ways, including a vigorous and devoted reliance on diversity events. At these events, Katherine "works the room" and makes it hers, taking advantage of the opportunity to meet with prospects, frequently converting them to clients. Katherine attends trade shows, conferences, luncheons, dinners, galas, and any other happenings with the potential to lead to new business connections.

When she attends a diversity event, Katherine is careful to take scrupulous notes on the people she meets and to follow up with every contact she's made. She sees these events as opportunities to put herself forward and impress potential clients with how Avail Workforce Management Solutions can help them. These events are no place to be shy, and Katherine is no shrinking violet. More than just putting herself forward, however, Katherine is a gentle if formidable sales representative for her company, not only initially but in the follow-up phase.

It is there, in the follow-up, that many others fall down, according to what Katherine hears. Others may introduce themselves with eager handshakes and glib chatter, but then they wait to hear back from these new contacts, hoping to turn them into conquests.

Not Katherine. She doesn't hope. She makes it happen. She doesn't wait. She takes action. Katherine excels in the follow-up—by phone, by e-mail, by snail mail with brochures and other literature, or by all of these in turn. She is the personification of the term *go-getter*—Katherine *goes* to events and *gets* new clients. And if her feet ache from walking, and her hand aches from shaking, and her jaw aches from talking up Avail, the pain is worth the gain in the form of new contacts made at the events and followed up thereafter.

One of Katherine's bibles is the book *Principled Networking* by Julia Hubbel, which is a mandatory read at Avail Workforce. The book's title might well have been written to describe Katherine, a serious, yet principled, advocate of networking. When she works the room at a diversity event, she spreads the story of her company and intrigues the people she most needs to reach.

But Katherine knows she needs to do more than dangle pretty promises to close a deal. She is obsessive about doing her homework, spending hours with her staff researching each prospective client. And she keeps an ear to the market to keep apprised of developments.

One of Katherine's most consistent approaches is to offer value-added solutions to her leads. A recent initiative she created, and proudly offers to all the contacts she makes at diversity events, is the Anserteam Network, an innovation that allows Avail to successfully compete with industry giants. Anserteam is a nationwide alliance of 40 independent staffing companies. Avail acts as their prime contractor when clients—often multinational companies—need to fill a large assignment. This could mean the need for instant placement of several hundred workers for one company, as might happen in the aftermath of a natural disaster such as Hurricane Katrina.

Of major significance is Avail's customized software that tracks all the temporary workers it places through the partnership—another selling point when Katherine's shaking hands at diversity events.

Katherine is also serious about mentoring other women, especially minority business owners. She helps them with certification issues, proposal writing, and maximizing networking opportunities with a focus on diversity events. Mentoring, she believes, is the true secret to success: "We women are not in competition. There is more than enough prosperity to go around. If you help others by mentoring them, you will discover that the universe is good to us when we are good to each other."

WHAT SHE ACHIEVED

As a young girl, Katherine lived in an apartment provided by the Atlanta Housing Authority. She watched her mother, of Cherokee heritage, struggle to survive. This proud, hardworking woman labored at three jobs, including cleaning other people's homes, to support the two of them. After seeing what her mom went through,

Katherine says, "I decided early on that I would find a way to improve the working lives of all mothers."

Katherine's life has a strong spiritual component and she believes that she did not randomly choose the workforce arena, but the profession chose her. It feels more like a calling than a career. Katherine passionately loves what she does. And that is the advice she gives to every woman she mentors and to every budding entrepreneur: "Be passionate about your business, work from your vision of the end result, and create a plan that will enable you to realize that vision. Do not let anyone or anything deter you."

In 2005, *Atlanta Woman* magazine recognized Katherine as Entrepreneur of the Year. *Fast Company* and the Women Presidents' Organization nominated her for its national 25 Women Who Are Changing the Game Award. And one of her most meaningful recognitions was being named to the *Inc.* 500 Fastest Growing Companies in America, where she joined the likes of Microsoft, Cisco, Starbuck's, and Oracle.

Today, Avail is recognized as the largest Native American company in the state of Georgia. Katherine's firm also ranks among the Top 100 Native American–Owned Businesses, the Top 500 Women-Owned Businesses, and the Top 500 Diversity-Owned Businesses in the United States.

But despite these well-deserved honors and awards, Katherine is most proud of her work on behalf of tribe members and minority women. She has created a partnership with the Atlanta Housing Authority to help low-income residents find jobs . . . and *futures*. Katherine is committed to convincing her Fortune clients that making their workplace more woman- and family-friendly is in their best interests.

And if there is a diversity event being held anywhere, you can be sure Katherine will be there, doing what she does best, meeting people, encouraging and helping people, and along the way bringing more business to Avail.

Market Your

Business for

Growth

Preparing for a Successful Sales Call

16

Most women think of a sales call as just that: the call. But a successful sales call really has three phases: *before, during,* and *after.* And over the years I've noticed that the *before*—the preparation—is often treated as the poor stepsister. Many women go into a sales call without any preparation at all, thinking they can just "chat" without investing up-front time in planning for the meeting.

Why do so many of us skip this step? We all can use the "lack of time" excuse, but I don't think that's the real reason. The real reason, I think, is that we don't know how to plan for a sales meeting, and, as a result, most of us just don't do it.

So hang on. You're about to learn the nuts and bolts of preparing for a sales call in five simple steps:

1. Research the prospect
2. Set meeting goals
3. Create a joint meeting agenda
4. Prepare your sales presentation
5. Assemble the right marketing materials

RESEARCH THE PROSPECT

With today's Web capability, there's no excuse for not investing the effort to find out about a business or individual prior to a sales call. Even if you only review the prospective company's Web site, you can gain a solid understanding of its goals, customers, physical reach, and offerings. And most public companies post their annual reports online so you can learn about their revenue and profitability.

At the least, you should understand the prospect's industry, offerings, customer base, corporate alliances, existing vendors for your product/service, and driving factors for your product/service.

In addition to Web research, don't overlook employees or clients who may have information or contacts in the prospect organization. As I do my premeeting research, I always shoot a quick e-mail to those I think may have connections or information on a prospect. You might be surprised to learn that your receptionist lives next door to the vice president of purchasing.

SET MEETING GOALS

After you complete your sales research, you're ready to set goals for your sales call. These goals will vary depending on your situation; however, with every sales call, I focus on three rather unusual goals. The great thing about these goals is that I've developed the habit of including them in my business conversations, so I no longer even have to think about them.

Understand the Prospect's Business and Industry

I want to better understand the business and industry of everyone I meet and this is most important with prospective clients. As an international speaker and columnist, I have the opportunity to meet women from across the country and around the world. Learning about their individual businesses and the sometimes quirky industries into which they fit is a real eye-opener. Over the years, I've gained a personal MBA just by questioning people and learning about their enterprises. So the first goal of my sales meeting always relates to understanding the prospect's business and industry.

Do the Prospect a Favor

I want to do one favor for everyone I meet. Now that may seem like an unusual goal, but here's a maxim that I live by: "I want everyone I know to owe me one favor." Why? Every time I do a favor for someone, my power in that relationship is strengthened. The more favors I do, the stronger my position in the relationship. If someone owes me a favor, I can call that marker in whenever I need it—whether it's for a business situation: "Can I ask you to introduce me to Jane Smith, the new vice president of purchasing?" or for a personal situation: "Could you make time for an informational interview with my son who is about to graduate from college?"

The interesting thing about my approach to favors is that once you are in this mind-set, you develop an ingrained habit that doesn't even require thought. You're always trying to figure out how you can do a favor for someone and, as a result, you continuously increase the balance in your "favor bank." So one of my goals for every sales call is to determine at least one immediate favor I can do for that individual.

Accept and Assign Next Steps

Over the years I've made my share of sales mistakes. I'm a Type A individual who often tries to shortcut situations, including planning. Some of my biggest blunders have occurred when I wasn't prepared to address follow-up at the conclusion of a meeting. So I always

- *create a few scenarios for* my *next step.* For example, after the meeting I might commit to the next step of submitting a short proposal or actually starting a project.
- *create a few scenarios for* the prospect's *next step.* For instance, the prospect could commit to calling one of my current clients as a reference. By ensuring that the prospect has at least one follow-up to the meeting, I keep her engaged in working with me.

CREATE A JOINT MEETING AGENDA

Although most of us use meeting agendas on a regular basis, we seldom do so for sales meetings. I've learned that creating a formal agenda that both you and the prospect have agreed on is a valuable tool.

I create and e-mail a joint meeting agenda to the prospect about a week in advance to gain her buy-in to our discussion topics and to request additional agenda items she might want to include.

Because very few salespeople use such an agenda, doing so will make you appear more organized and competent, differentiating you from the competition while demonstrating you value your prospect's time. Above all, this agenda makes prospects feel more integrated into the sales call and, as a result, you'll have fewer cancellations or postponements.

PREPARE YOUR SALES PRESENTATION

After you've completed your research on the prospect organization, you should have a sense of how your company can help this prospect. But don't make the mistake of thinking of your presentation as a sales pitch; think of it as a two-way conversation that will allow you to uncover questions, issues, and needs that your prospect may have. We'll discuss the nitty-gritty of the sales presentation in the next chapter, but keep in mind that the purpose is not to pitch your offering, but to help your prospect see your value to its business.

ASSEMBLE THE RIGHT MARKETING MATERIALS

Your final step in preparing for a sales call is determining which marketing materials and other information you should bring.

Gather Existing Materials

I often bring the items in the list that follows, but I may bring other material depending on the situation:

- My business card (of course!)
- Articles I've written that demonstrate my expertise and capability
- Brochures or one-sheet flyers about my firm

When deciding what to bring, I always focus on the prospect. I want my material to show that I am an expert in achieving the results that she needs, so I may customize my brochures or flyers to focus on my expertise in her industry or with companies of her size.

Although I may have already mailed or e-mailed a certain marketing piece to a prospect, I always bring a printed copy along on the sales call. I've already mentioned an article I wrote about certification for *Fast Company* magazine a few years back. This article is posted on my Web site and I distribute it to prospects through an e-mail link. Depending on the situation, I may also send the PDF version as an attachment. Regardless of whether or not I've already sent this electronically, I put a copy of it into every package I mail and every package I take to a sales meeting.

Why do I do this? There are two reasons.

First of all, I assume that most women entrepreneurs are like me. They're busy. Depending on the kind of day I'm having, I may access a link . . . or not. I may open a file . . . or not. But if I receive a printed version during a sales meeting, I'm going to at least glance at it.

Second, I had the *Fast Company* article professionally printed and it looks great. I gained the magazine's approval to use its logo next to mine at the top of the article, so I'm going to use this piece whenever I can.

Create New Sales Materials Quickly

What if you're just starting out and have no marketing materials? That's the situation I was in when I began my current business. So I interviewed my prospects about the biggest problems they were facing and wrote my proposed solutions to these problems. I then created a four-color template with my logo and printed these solutions on the template. These solution sheets worked like a charm and became the basis for my formal marketing materials.

And here's an approach that always gains attention: I take photos of the results I have achieved. For example, after I helped one of my clients gain a contract with Volvo, I took a picture of her standing next to a large Volvo sign. And I did the same thing with a client after I worked with her to gain the national Pizza Hut account.

How do I use these pictures?

I incorporate them into a marketing sheet that I e-mail prior to a sales call and then also print out to bring with me to the meeting. And when I do PowerPoint presentations as part of a sales call, I include these pictures and tell the success stories that I've achieved for my clients.

Regardless of the type of materials you create, keep in mind that the worst thing you can do is to present materials that look "homemade" or unprofessional. Above all else, you *must* demonstrate that you and your business are top-shelf.

■ **MENTOR:**	*Helene B. Gralnick*
■ **BUSINESS:**	*Chico's FAS, Inc. (Chico's)*
■ **LOCATION:**	*Fort Myers, Florida, U.S.A.*
■ **INDUSTRY:**	*Retail Clothing*

ONE WOMAN WHO DID IT RIGHT

Raised in Miami, Helene Gralnick was the epitome of a Florida girl, spending her days outdoors swimming, sailing, and biking. Then, while earning a degree in Elementary Education, Helene became fascinated with the philosophies of Maria Montessori. By studying Montessori's approach, she came to understand that the secret to success was to ensure that people were comfortable and happy. Helene would later apply this approach not to education but to the world of business, where she would focus on making her customers comfortable and happy.

After graduating from the University of Miami, Helene embarked on a trip to Mexico that was to change her life. In Guadalajara she met her future husband, Marvin. Up to that point, he had been designing leather jackets and accessories, but the two of them decided there was a market for both his unique designs as well as the local folk art. So they invested $1,500 in a beat-up van and began driving back and forth to the States, selling their wares to retail stores.

In 1983, they decided to open a store of their own. With a loan from Helene's mother, the couple acquired an 800-square-foot storefront on Sanibel Island. They decided to call their store "Chico's" after a friend's bilingual parrot, and gave it the full name of "Chico's Folk Art Specialties."

Although he wasn't a carpenter, Marvin outfitted the store himself using inexpensive wood the couple scrounged around to buy. Helene then invested the money they had saved on building materials to create an environment that would appeal to their customers' senses. In the days of stale department store air and Muzak, Helene filled the air with sandalwood essential oils and played upbeat music. So women could shop leisurely without feeling guilty, she set up a "husband's chair" and provided handmade wooden toys and puzzles for children to play with. The ultimate result was just what Helene intended—the store was filled with positive energy . . . and lots of customers.

In those early days, Chico's was very much the Gralnick's family store. Their children, Rio and Sarah, got off the school bus at the store, marking their arrival with a trail of jackets and books from the front of the store to the back. After a quick snack, they'd go outside where Helene kept an eye on them playing under their "Magic Tree." Because money was tight and preprinted bags were expensive, the kids wrote "Chico's" on hundreds of plain brown bags. Then, to add a personal touch, they tied brightly colored ribbons on every bag that left the store. Chico's reputation began to grow as tourists spread the word about the charming family who ran the unique island store.

Although Chico's initially focused on Mexican folk art, that all changed when Helene and Marvin bought a truckload of cotton sweaters and watched them fly off the shelves. Following their customers' lead, they changed their focus from folk art to sweaters, and then evolved to other items of women's clothing. To reflect this change, they shortened the name to "Chico's FAS" and 12-year-old Rio developed their first slogan: "Chico's—A Reputation You Can Wear."

During those first few years, Helene considered a day with $500 in sales as wildly successful. The family even went out to dinner to celebrate such days. But before long, every day became a "$500 day."

And then they began to ring up $1,000 days. And Chico's grew and grew.

HOW SHE DID IT

From the beginning, Helene's intent was to remove all sales pressure. She never pushed customers to make a purchase; she just wanted them to feel comfortable so they would come back time and again. By creating this kind of atmosphere, her customers *did* come back, and they *did buy.*

Beginning with the first store, Helene wanted Chico's to be an important part of the community. She spoke at local fashion shows and then brought the women back to the store. And when she and Marvin decided to expand to the second floor of their building, they created a children's art contest called "Chico's Breaks Through" to involve the entire community in their expansion.

Helene's approach to growth was simple: Determine which items customers liked and then stock and restock those items. She knew intuitively which new items would be hot and delighted in stocking items customers could not find elsewhere. As a result of Helene's merchandising savvy, Chico's quickly outgrew its expanded space, so the Gralnicks acquired a second location that served as a warehouse and office, as well as a store. The second store was within walking distance of the first, so to encourage customers to visit both stores, they created a different layout for this store. And as they built store three and then four, rather than taking a cookie-cutter approach, they made each store a little different—inspiring customers to visit them all.

To promote their unique stores, Helene devised creative promotional materials. Continuing her practice of community involvement, she enlisted the elementary school's art teacher to sketch a few items. She had those printed on brown paper and sat down with her kids to fold and stamp the pages. That "family style" mailing was the precursor to Chico's wildly successful loyalty program, the Passport Club, launched in 1991. Beginning with that first mailing, the elements of the program have evolved over the years and now include a monthly catalog mailed to millions of women.

By joining the Passport Club, a customer chooses to receive this monthly mailing. Every issue of the catalog is photographed on-site at an exotic location, allowing women to envision themselves in the dramatic flowing clothing. When developing the catalog, and the clothing in general, Helene focused on how women wanted to feel, because she recognized that to look good, you must feel good. So she and her design staff put themselves in the place of customers and went through a questioning process: "It is Sunday morning; what do you want to wear?" "You're going out to lunch with friends; how do you want to look?" "It's Saturday night and you're going out for a casual dinner; what color do you feel like wearing?"

While this ongoing communication hit the mark with customers, Chico's really skyrocketed in 1997 with the introduction of new fabrics and new designs. Rather than the standard 2 to 16 sizing, Chico's has long used the more forgiving 0, 1, 2, and 3, which better fits the minds and bodies of their target 35- to 55-year-old women. This sizing, coupled with its unique stretchable fabric, sent a message of *comfortable elegance* in a world of tight-fitting, trendy clothes.

Although Helene recently retired, it was her knack for design and concept that drove Chico's product innovation. The Gralnicks' design strengths, business savvy, and relentless focus on the customer allowed them to launch this dynamic company that even today carries on Helene's original intention of making every customer comfortable and happy.

WHAT SHE ACHIEVED

The little business that started out in a single storefront had grown to 75 stores when the Gralnicks took their company public in 1993. And today it has expanded to 763 retail locations. Virtually all the company's clothing, jewelry, and accessories are designed by an in-house product development team and bear the distinctive "Chico's" trademark.

Helene credits her amazing success to simply loving what she did. Over all those years, she never once said she was "going to work"; she always said she was "going to Chico's." By "going to Chico's" she was able to combine her zest for life, love of art, and knack for style to develop the unique brand that is a favorite of women across the country. To this day, Helene smiles every time she hears a customer use the word "love" to describe Chico's clothing and the Chico's experience.

In addition to the rewards of their business, Helene and Marvin also received some of the most sought-after accolades in the world of commerce. In 1993, they won the coveted Ernst & Young Entrepreneur of the Year Award, recognizing their amazing accomplishment in building Chico's from the ground up. And in the turbulent and trying business years of both 2001 and 2002, Chico's was named Forbes #1 Best Small Company.

Although retail sales can be a challenging arena, Chico's continues to thrive. Beginning with their first little store, their success has rested on paying attention to the customer. From the initial transition from folk art to sweaters, Helene's achievements, and those of Chico's, relied on being not so much in the apparel business as in the people business. Even today, Helene uses her team members, who she fondly refers to as "Chiccettes," as a barometer of Chico's success. And she delights when women who have been with the company for more than 20 years say, "The bigger we get . . . the stronger we get . . . the better we get."

The Chico's story is one of passion and creativity and love, and the products are almost secondary. Oh sure, women visit these stores to buy great clothes, but Chico's *aficionados* go to experience something else as well—something that Helene envisioned from the start—an environment that makes every customer and team member feel comfortable and happy.

Conducting a Successful Sales Call

17

You've done a lot of things right to get to the sales call, so let's look at what you can do during the actual meeting to come away a winner.

First of all, remember the old sales adage: "All things being equal, people want to do business with friends. All things being not so equal, people *still* want to do business with friends." Building a friendly relationship with a prospect is the first step in developing the confidence and trust that are at the heart of every sale. When I'm on a sales call, I don't ever move into business mode until I've created an attitude of friendship. The arrival and introduction phase is, in my opinion, the most important segment of your sales presentation; if you botch this, you might as well go home.

ARRIVE WITH ENERGY

As far as I'm concerned, Emmy award–winning producer Heidi Berenson, now president of Berenson Communications, Inc., is the Empress of Presentation. Heidi harnesses her network television experience to coach top executives on the presentation techniques of television. Chief among them? High energy and passion—which are contagious. And in no situation is that more beneficial than in a sales call.

I always try to arrive early for a sales call to spend a few minutes with the receptionist or administrative assistant. I've found that these folks can really support your efforts before, during, and after the sales meeting. They are often a good source of current information such as what key issues the decision makers are dealing with.

How do you discover this information? It's simple: Just ask.

I typically ask an upbeat question like, "Jane, what's the most exciting thing happening in your department (or within the company) these days?" And Jane will then often tell me something that will open the door to further questions. Then I'll generally be able to use that information in my presentation.

BE MEMORABLE

Over the years, I've pitched to groups of all sizes, from a single woman in a home office to a group of 47 Hewlett-Packard executives. Products and services being equal, I've found that there are two ways to differentiate yourself and your company from the rest of the pack: Stand up and get them laughing.

Get Up on Your Feet

I always try to stand during my presentations; the only exception is when I present to an individual in a wheelchair.

Why stand?

Millions of dollars of research proves that it makes a difference. A study from the Wharton School of the University of Pennsylvania indicates that your close rate can increase by 21 percent if you stand while presenting. And further research from the University of Minnesota found that customers are willing to pay 26 percent more for a product or service that is sold to them by someone who is standing versus seated.

Since discovering this research, I've developed the habit of standing to make sales presentations. And believe me it really does make a difference. Why? By standing, an individual commands attention, authority, and interest. And this is particularly true for women.

Several years ago I presented to a group of John Deere executives. When I walked into the room, eight men in dark suits and white shirts were staring back at me with looks that said, "What's this little girl going to tell us?"

As you may have experienced yourself, presenting to an all-male audience can be tough. And as a woman running your own business, you're in a particularly vulnerable position speaking to some groups of men. But I've found that standing while presenting to them, even if there are only two or three in the group, makes a real difference in my sense of command and results in an increase in attention and respect. (By the way, I *did* close that deal with John Deere.)

Standing is easy enough to do when you are presenting to a group, but how do you stand in a one-on-one situation without seeming presumptuous?

Well, I always find an excuse to stand. I look for a whiteboard to write on or sometimes even bring my own flip chart with graphics or notes that require me to stand while discussing. By standing, you come across as an expert, an authority figure, someone who really knows her stuff.

Get Them Laughing

I *insist* on having fun. And sales presentations are no exception. Unless you are selling funeral services, there is always room for fun in sales. I've an advantage over many of you, for I sell and present exclusively to women, so I can sprinkle "chick" humor into my presentations. One of my favorites is the story of how my Ya-Ya Sisters and I have given each other names. (My Ya-Ya name is The Countess Who Wants It All, because I do want it all, not only for myself, but for every other woman in business!)

What kind of humor would work for your audience?

Perhaps you can hone some industry or regional humor. Of course, you never want to be condescending or insulting in any way. But, I promise, if you work at incorporating humor into your sales presentations, you will absolutely differentiate yourself from the pack.

Think of it, don't you want to buy from and work with someone who is fun?

FOLLOW THIS FORMULA

Enough about logistics, let's talk about the presentation itself. If you're like me, you love to talk, but that can be a great way to kill a sale. So let me teach you my 75 Percent Rule:

I listen 75 percent of the time; I talk 25 percent of the time.

I work to stay within these boundaries and the more I stick to this rule, the greater my sales success. Remember my key formula: Listen, Listen, Listen, Talk. Rinse. Repeat.

Use My Eight-Step Formula

Based on the fact that I'm only going to do 25 percent of the talking, here's my eight-step formula for every sales call:

1. *Create rapport.* Like any conversation, you'll introduce yourself and get to know those you're presenting to. As women, most of us are really good at this because we've spent a large part of our lives building relationships. So this comes easy to us. But remember the 75 Percent Rule and let your prospect do most of the talking.
2. *Establish credibility.* After I feel I'm in synch with my prospect, I'll say something like, "I'm anxious to learn all I can about your company, and before we do that could I share just a bit about my organization?" Then I give the prospect a brief overview. During this overview, I include names of individuals and companies within the prospect's industry for whom my company has done work. This gives her an immediate sense that I'm an insider in her industry.
3. *Provide a benefit sound bite.* My goal at this point is to make my prospect aware of the benefits she will receive from working with me. One of my benefit sound bites might be, "I'm going to show you how I help women entrepreneurs gain new Fortune customers." Or "I'll explain how I introduce women like you into new strategic accounts."

4. *Determine needs.* If you've done your homework, you'll come into the meeting understanding the business and industry, as well as the firm's problems and goals. Use that information as your baseline and begin to ask questions about the prospect's individual problems and goals. At this point, ask short, open-ended questions and LISTEN to the answers.

5. *Provide examples of success.* This is the most crucial part of the formula. Here you sift through all the information you've obtained and address each issue, providing examples of your past success in each area. My prospect's eyes light up when I say something like, "Pat, I know you've been trying to gain a foothold in the communications industry. I'd love to have you meet my client Jodi Elkins of SpectraWorld. In the six months that we've been working together, we've closed deals with both SBC and BellSouth." From here, I tell a memorable story of how Jodi and I landed a big contract for her company. A story like this allows me to paint a picture that my prospect can relate to and remember.

6. *Answer questions.* It's important to provide compelling answers to the prospect's questions. While doing this, I ensure I'm on track by continually asking, "Did I explain that clearly?" or "What other questions do you have about that?" As questions arise, I address them one by one. I've found the best way to answer tough questions is by providing examples of how I've solved similar problems for other clients.

7. *Summarize outcomes and action items.* As you begin to close the meeting, summarize your key points and be sure you agree on follow-up items. While you'll likely take on a few action items such as providing a proposal, it's important that your prospect also agrees to at least one item so she stays connected to the follow-up process.

8. *Ask for the business.* This is the step where we most often fail. So many of you tell me that you feel great up to this point and then you fall apart. The word that I most commonly hear is that you feel "uncomfortable" asking for the sale.

Because this is such a universal challenge, I'm going to devote an entire chapter (Chapter 19) to "Closing the Deal."

■ **MENTOR:**	*Sepi Asefnia*
■ **BUSINESS:**	*SEPI Engineering Group, Inc.*
■ **LOCATION:**	*Raleigh, North Carolina, U.S.A.*
■ **INDUSTRY:**	*Transportation Engineering and Planning*

ONE WOMAN WHO DID IT RIGHT

Born in Tehran, Iran, at a time when women were fighting for equality, Sepi Asefnia was not raised in a traditional Iranian family. While growing up, Sepi observed her female friends learning to cook, sew, and manage a household. While she valued the contributions of homemakers, Sepi's goals in life were very different. Inspired by the capabilities of her mother, an educator and independent woman, and despite the norms of her society, Sepi dreamt of earning a university degree and becoming an independent businesswoman.

In 1978, Sepi faced one of the most difficult of challenges: watching her family divide. Her brother was sent to the United States to attend college, shortly followed by her sister, and then by Sepi herself. Although she had intended to return home at some point, that was not to be. Because of the political upheaval and abdication of the Shah, Sepi and her siblings no longer were allowed to return to Iran.

Despite her family challenges and her limited English at the time, Sepi was able to earn degrees in both Agricultural Engineering and Civil Engineering from North Carolina State University. She then spent 15 years in transportation engineering, a field that she loved. With encouragement from her family and friends, she decided to establish SEPI Engineering Group in May of 2001. Since that time, Sepi has expanded her firm, continually adding new engineering disciplines to create the full-service civil engineering firm it is today.

Sepi has capitalized on the fact that she is a woman entrepreneur in a male-dominated industry. She is continually told that she brings a fresh perspective to the transportation engineering industry, and she believes this is because women are intuitive communicators with a personal touch. She believes this "personal touch" has helped her grow her business, particularly in sales.

HOW SHE DID IT

Soft-spoken and feminine, Sepi Asefnia is the antithesis of a pushy salesperson. But, as the president of an engineering firm that supports public- and private-sector clients, Sepi knows that selling is a critical component of business success.

When she first started her business, Sepi worked out of her home. With low overhead and fewer constraints than larger firms, she was able to provide proposals that were flexible in price and remarkable in quality. To establish credibility, she worked incredibly hard to produce high-quality results at reasonable prices. She made it a point to go above and beyond every client request. Her philosophy was not just to "get the job done," but to study how each project would affect the safety and welfare of the surrounding community. And after a while, she became known for this.

Over the years, Sepi has learned that relationships are the key to winning sales. Because the sales cycle for her projects can be very long—sometimes years—she has discovered that success is about developing and maintaining those relationships. As a result of her reputation for completing projects successfully, she now regularly receives opportunities to bid on high-profile projects. But this wasn't always the case.

In the beginning, Sepi thought a sales call was about making a pitch rather than establishing a relationship. When she had the opportunity to present her business, she would shake hands and launch into her company's capabilities. Rather than just sitting down and getting to know her prospect, she would make a hard sales pitch about what SEPI Engineering could do.

After much trial and error, she now knows what's important. Because of her unique background, she finds people want to know things like, "Where were you born?" and "Why did you decide to start your own business?" She loves to answer these questions, because she realizes this is a way to develop a relationship with her prospect. As a result, they get to know her, remember her, and feel comfortable picking up the phone to give her a call.

Sepi also learned that you have to be alert during a sales call and "read" your prospect well. You can't just go in with a set agenda and be intent on sticking to it. Even though you have an appointment, something important could have come up to distract your prospect, or you might just be catching him or her at a busy time. So she's learned to be reactive to the situation rather than trying to force her agenda.

Sepi suggests a good way to hone your sales skills is to pay attention to how others sell to you. Notice what you like or dislike in a salesperson's approach and try to modify your presentation skills based on this. One of her hard rules is to never take a relationship for granted, because you just don't know where your next opportunity may come from. She remembers staying in touch with a friend from college. Then, when she was launching her business, she called him. He was excited that she was starting her own firm and recommended her to a big contractor, which resulted in a breakthrough contract for her company.

In addition to relationships, Sepi believes that a real key to sales is belief in the capabilities of your company. You must feel at a gut level that you are the best provider of what you are selling. You must do a great job in every presentation so you stand out in your prospects' minds. This doesn't mean that you will close every deal, but you will win eventually.

WHAT SHE ACHIEVED

Sepi is living proof that a woman-owned engineering firm can develop a niche and provide its clients with services that equal and surpass those of the engineering "guys."

She started her business from scratch. And her sheer determination coupled with an ability to build relationships gained the loyal clients she needed to establish herself in the industry. Today she continues to work with these clients and has added many others. Now in its fifth year, SEPI Engineering Group, Inc., has become one of the top firms of its kind in the region.

Over the past several years, Sepi has built a solid niche both inside her industry and within her geographic region. She was designated the North Carolina Employer of the Year by the Women's Transportation Seminar. She's also received the YWCA Academy of Women Award in Science & Technology and was named one of the Top 25 Women in Business by her region's business journal.

When she founded her company, no established network existed for women working in the transportation industry, so Sepi joined organizations such as the WPO and NAWBO, where she learned to reach out to other women business owners for advice, and to help them as well. Through a mentoring program for engineering students of local universities, Sepi works with one female engineering student at a time in her office. She supports and guides that student through her career decisions and helps her gain industry knowledge.

Today, Sepi's goal is to be a role model for her daughter and other young girls. She wants to show them that women can be successful leaders in traditionally male-dominated fields. And she's proven that's true.

Asking Good
Sales Questions

18

Questions are your most important sales tool, and the kinds of questions you ask in a sales call can really set you apart you from your competition.

OVERCOME THESE MISTAKES
WHEN ASKING QUESTIONS

I often accompany my clients on sales calls to help them improve their presentations and, over the years, I've noticed that those less seasoned in sales make two consistent mistakes when asking questions.

Don't Rush to React

After asking an individual question, many women are so anxious to present their business that they provide a knee-jerk reaction to their prospect's response. For example, if a prospect comments that he has been frustrated with long delivery times, you may want to launch into a stream of conversation about how your customers continually compliment you on your quick delivery times. Or when a prospect mentions that his current contractor does a sloppy job of cleanup, you might begin to detail how daily cleanup is one of your company's top priorities.

While these immediate responses may seem to make sense, in effect they make prospects feel as though they are being interrogated or "pitched" to. Quick turnaround responses make you appear to be a pushy salesperson rather than an expert in your field who has the prospect's interests at heart.

If you can discipline yourself to make notes about your prospect's complaints and just sit on them at this point in the conversation, you'll see the greater clout your responses can wield later in the meeting.

Find the Real Answer

Women with less sales experience often accept superficial answers, rather than probing down for the "real" answers. So when a prospect says she is concerned about the level of overtime her employees have been working, you may ask "why" and she might comment that new orders have jumped but she hasn't been able to hire new line personnel quickly enough. The "real" question then is *why* she can't staff up to address the problem.

When you get the answer to *that* question, you should try to go even deeper to determine not only the business impact but also the personal impact that situation has on her. You might ask questions such as, "What are the cost implications of this situation?" and "How have your employees reacted to this overtime?" And to determine the personal impact, "What kind of hours have you, personally, been putting in to deal with this?" and "How has being overstretched prevented you from doing other important things?"

Moving to this level of questions allows you to truly understand the situation, and also helps the prospect see the problem in a different, usually more intense, light.

BECOME A SALES QUESTIONING PRO

You want your prospect to view you as an expert in your field—someone who really knows what she is doing and how to get it done. To achieve this, you need to ask two types of questions: credibility questions and qualifying questions.

Let's look at both of these.

Ask Credibility Questions

A great way to demonstrate your expertise and engage your prospects is to ask them to talk about problems they've had with your industry. For example, if you own a travel agency, ask about their last business trip. What was the booking process? The results? Were things done quickly and easily? Did everything happen on the trip exactly as they had expected? If not, what went wrong? Why did that happen? What did their travel agency do to correct it?

Listen for problems. But, remember, this isn't the time for knee-jerk reactions to each of their responses. Instead, make notes of their problems and issues so you can discuss them later in your conversation.

By asking intelligent, well-thought-out credibility questions, you show the prospect that you are an expert in your industry. For example, when helping a woman determine whether to certify her woman-owned business, I ask questions like:

- How did you become aware of certification?
- Have any of your customers asked you to become certified?
- Are any of your competitors certified?
- What value do you think certification will bring to your business?
- What do you, personally, hope to gain from becoming certified?
- Is there any other way that certification could help you?
- How do you plan to complete the certification process?
- How long do you expect it will take to complete the process?

The purpose of credibility questions is to get my prospect thinking about her need for my offering. At the same time, I want her to feel confident that my organization is not only capable of delivering this service, but, hopefully, is the only organization that can deliver *exactly* what she needs and wants *right now.*

Ask Qualifying Questions

After you've established yourself as an expert, you're ready to ask qualifying questions. The better you qualify the situation, the greater your chances of winning this prospect over as a customer.

In a sales situation, you should ask primarily open-ended questions. Many questions are specific to your industry and you'll have to determine what those are. But here are some qualifying questions you might consider as a start:

- How urgent is this problem?
- How important is this problem?
- What approaches have you already tried?
- What resources do you have to get this done?
- What does your budget look like for this segment?
- How much do you plan to invest in the entire effort?
- How soon do you think you'll be ready to start?
- What do you think this is worth to your organization?
- What is this worth to you personally?
- What will happen if you fail at this effort?

RECAP THEIR ANSWERS

Of course, as your prospect responds to any question, you'll be taking notes. And, after you obtain responses to each group of questions—first credibility and then qualifying—you should stop and recap.

Here is my recap script:

- If I heard you correctly this is the situation . . .
- These are the problems (or opportunities) in that situation . . .
- I believe this is what you need to accomplish . . .
- It seems as though this is the cost (or value) to your organization of this situation . . .

The purpose of recapping her answers is to be sure that you and the prospect are on the same wavelength, and to get her to see the full scope of the problem or opportunity.

WORK WITH THE DECISION MAKER

The larger the organization, the more layers you have to cut through to get to the real decision maker. That's one of the reasons I *love* working exclusively with women entrepreneurs, because I know I'm *always* dealing with the real decision maker.

You can ask many questions to determine the real decision maker, but there is definitely a right way and a wrong way to go about this. Be careful to AVOID the following questions, for they can easily insult or belittle your prospect, and ruin any chances of making a sale:

- Who makes these decisions?
- Who besides you will be making the decision?
- Who else in your organization should I be discussing this with?

However, if your goal is for your prospect to become your ally, try my approach. In the series of questions that follow, note that I use the phrase "our ideas" to reflect my joint partnership with the prospect:

- Jane, tell me about your decision-making process?
- Who specifically will you discuss our ideas with?
- How do you plan to present our ideas to them?
- How do you think they'll react to our ideas?
- Do you see any reasons that they might nix our ideas?
- What do you think we can do to bring them over to our side?

MOVE FROM QUESTIONS TO CLOSE

After asking good sales questions, taking notes while listening to the responses, recapping the responses, and joining forces to reach decision makers, you'll be ready to move on to the close.

■ **MENTOR:**	*Sharon P. Whiteley*
■ **BUSINESS:**	*ThirdAge, Inc.*
■ **LOCATION:**	*Boston, Massachusetts, U.S.A.*
■ **INDUSTRY:**	*Online Media, Research, and Marketing*

ONE WOMAN WHO DID IT RIGHT

Sharon P. Whiteley—business leader, private investor, and author—is CEO of ThirdAge, Inc., an online content, marketing, and research company serving dynamic baby boomers and marketers who want to reach them. A seasoned entrepreneur, Sharon has been the driving force behind ThirdAge.com, which has close to one million members and is the premier online destination for "midlifers"—adults in their 40s, 50s, 60s, and beyond.

Prior to ThirdAge, Sharon founded and built five other innovative companies in the retail industry. Among her notable projects is Boston's Faneuil Hall Marketplace where she conceived the pushcart concept of transitory retail that has become a staple in today's shopping centers.

A recipient of numerous leadership and business awards, Sharon was one of the first 15 women to receive the Entrepreneur of the Year Award sponsored by Ernst & Young. An enthusiastic champion of women entrepreneurs, she was a founding partner in 8Wings Ventures LLC, an early-stage private equity investment group. This interest led her to coauthor *The Old Girls' Network: Insider Advice for Women Building Businesses in a Man's World*, a how-to book for aspiring entrepreneurs.

A charismatic and dynamic business leader, Sharon routinely mentors and supports other women and their enterprises. She believes that women, by virtue of their innate understanding of human nature and skill in building relationships, are perfectly positioned to excel in sales.

HOW SHE DID IT

Sharon Whiteley believes an average salesperson *tells;* a good salesperson *explains;* an excellent salesperson *demonstrates;* but a truly gifted salesperson *inspires* a prospect so much that she sells herself on the idea.

One of Sharon's earliest and most instructive sales experiences revolved around her idea to lease vendor pushcarts throughout Faneuil Hall, a specialty retail shopping center in Boston. Sharon's idea was driven by a looming, grand-opening-day deadline. In a nutshell, temporary retail activity needed to be added to the spacious, unoccupied glass-canopied greenhouses along both sides of the famed Quincy Market. Although pushcart vendors appear in every mall today, at the time this was a novel concept that took a bit of selling. First Sharon had to persuade the management team at Faneuil Hall that it would not only work, but, more important, it would flourish.

Before her first sales presentation, Sharon met with the owners to discuss every aspect of concern, their specific issues, and their aspirations for the project. During this initial discovery process she planned and asked five critical questions:

1. What was their vision for the development?
2. What was their greatest concern about achieving this vision?
3. How did they want to differentiate this project from others in their portfolio?
4. How did they envision the experience for visitors of the Marketplace?
5. If they could eliminate one problem, what would it be?

The reaction of the owners was very positive because no one had ever asked the kinds of questions that led them to really define the essence of the project; and they later told Sharon that her questions added immense value. She left the meeting not only elated, but also with the resources necessary to fashion a compelling solution.

What she learned was that the developers wanted this pioneering urban center to be the crown jewel of their company; they wanted it to be a unique, fun, and upbeat customer experience. Their greatest concern was the empty and highly visible glass building wings. The key to discovering this information was Sharon's use of thoughtful, provocative, *high-return* questions, and the outcome exceeded her expectations. On the grand opening day, 52 specialty pushcart merchants opened for business under the moniker, the Bull Market, and retail history was made.

Over the years, Sharon has learned the value of high-return questions. These questions are markedly different from closed-end questions that enable the responder to answer with one word, a number, or a short phrase. Sharon uses high-return questions for specific information and fact-finding. For example, "Do you control the buying decisions for your department?" or "How many people do you need to move through your facility in an hour?" or "Who are your competitors?"

As a great salesperson, Sharon recognizes that high-return questions invite participation in the process and help pave the way to increasingly expansive responses. Using such questions requires her prospect to evaluate, analyze, speculate, or express feelings. As a result, Sharon is able to gain valuable information about a customer's needs, and she fosters trust—the roadway to a lasting relationship.

Asking questions, both inside and outside an organization, is extremely valuable. It has become part of the operating culture at ThirdAge and is encouraged among all levels of the company. Sharon focuses on questions because of the benefits they provide:

Questions provide a chance to learn. You learn when you're listening, not when you're talking. Questions can prompt the prospect or customer to share information critical to making the sale.

Questions give you a chance to listen. Questions are the most underrated and underused element of communication. When you ask a question that encourages a prospect to speak at length—especially about a topic pertinent to your opportunity—you learn and build trust at the same time.

Questions can position you as a real contributor. By asking quality, high-return questions, you gain credibility in the eyes of your prospect. Asking general and closed-end questions, such as "How many people work here?" falls short of the rich information you will glean from asking, "How are you doing in terms of finding and keeping good people? Do you use a particular strategy?"

Questions help you keep the process moving. Checking in and asking your customer or prospect if she has any questions, concerns, or is interested in more information along the way ensures that you haven't lost your connection with the customer.

Questions can uncover data critical to the sale. You can often learn more about your competition from your prospects and customers than from any other single source. Customer impressions of competitive offerings can allow you to keep tabs on your competitors.

Questions can lead to referrals. Asking for and getting referrals can be one of the most valuable parts of your sales and marketing plan. To put it simply, if you ask for a referral, you may get one; if you never ask, you almost certainly won't.

Your most important question? Ask for the sale! Don't ever leave a sales meeting of any kind without asking for the sale. As the saying goes, "If you don't ask, you don't get."

WHAT SHE ACHIEVED

Today, as CEO of ThirdAge, Sharon's early Quincy Marketplace lessons still hold true. As a media property, Sharon's firm continually seeks ways to differentiate itself, ways to promote leading-edge content, and ways to keep its site exciting and relevant.

To make this happen, her team needs to identify and engage leading authors, topical experts, and major thought leaders to contribute their knowledge to the ThirdAge site and become part of its "Expert Team." These special contributors are compensated with prominent media exposure on the ThirdAge.com Web site. Because this is not the traditional way writers are remunerated, Sharon's team often must enroll them in the ThirdAge vision. One of the ways they accomplish this and build meaningful relationships starts with—you guessed it—asking high-return questions.

Sharon believes that improving your selling game starts with asking thoughtful, high-value questions because when you let your interest, natural curiosity, and enthusiasm shine through, good things invariably happen.

Today, Sharon's current business, ThirdAge, has close to one million members. And it is gaining great traction as the Web site of choice for people in their 40s, 50s, and 60s who are redefining what it means to get older. Sharon is proud of ThirdAge, and knows that her organization's ability to learn from her early career lessons has contributed to the company's success.

As for the Bull Market, it continues to flourish in busy Quincy Market, and her pushcart retail model continues to be emulated in shopping landscapes everywhere. Were it not for Sharon's early questioning days at the Faneuil Hall Marketplace and the knowledge gained as a result, the opportunity to innovate, create, and perform would not have been optimized. She is certain of that.

Closing the Deal

19

Let's face it girls, women have a reputation as weak closers. Because many of us were raised to be sweet, kind, and considerate, our prospects often assume they can take advantage of us. Well, here is where you can turn a negative into a positive. Let people think what they will while you develop good closing skills to capitalize on their expectation of your weakness.

BECOME A "GOOD CLOSER"

Being a good closer doesn't mean that you turn into an aggressive witch. Just the opposite is true. I always think about what I am selling from the perspective of how it will help others. If I believe something will add real value then I ask myself "How DARE I not share this with her and convince her of the value it will bring to her business?" This reflects back to my earlier comments that sales is about the customer rather than about *you*.

So what, exactly, are the components of closing a deal?

Well, my take on this is a little different from what you might have learned elsewhere. I think of a sales presentation in two segments: an opening and a closing.

Everything you've done up to this point—conducting research, developing and delivering a solid presentation, asking and answering questions—everything to this point is the opening.

Now you're ready for the close. And just as your opening didn't all happen in a single meeting—remember you conducted your research and developed your presentation before you arrived at the prospect's location—your close doesn't all necessarily happen in a single meeting. Oh, if you're lucky it may, but don't feel like a failure if you need to return to meet with the client, sometimes more than once, to close the deal.

The three key components of closing are: handling objections, presenting a proposal, and negotiating. So let's look at these three components.

HANDLE OBJECTIONS

At times, you won't have to deal with any objections. You may just present your offering and your price and your prospect will just sign away. This actually happens more often than you might think, provided you do a great job of your opening tasks.

But assuming that's not the case, let's discuss handling objections.

Over the years, I've created a list of the most common objections my prospects raise in a sales call and at least three different responses to each of them. For example, I recently met with a client headquartered in Washington to discuss how I could help her apply for WBENC certification and then market her business to national corporations I knew would be interested. After some discussion, she commented that certification would not be a good fit for her company for she was only doing business in the Northwest and not across the United States. Her objection gave me the opportunity to explain that, like her, most of my clients were regional. And I had helped them complete the certification process and had, indeed, enabled them to gain new customers in their regions and then expand across the country. Then I gave her a few specific examples. I was glad that she had raised this objection, because if she had kept it under her hat, I wouldn't have been aware of her concern and wouldn't have been able to address it.

I always think of objections as just a call for more information—another opportunity to get closer to a "yes." But to move in that direction, you must be prepared to respond to objections, so take the time to think through the top three objections you consistently hear and develop your responses to them.

PRESENT YOUR PROPOSAL

After you address objections, you're ready for the proposal. There will be times when you can make a verbal proposal on the spot and times when your prospect will require a written proposal. Each of these has its benefits.

Present a Verbal Proposal

A verbal proposal allows you to shorten the sales cycle and close a deal quicker, accelerating the revenue flow from a new client. As a result of my preliminary research, I go into a meeting with some sense of what I can do for a prospect. But I almost always modify these ideas based on our conversation. I never make the assumption that my verbal proposal will be exactly what the prospect needs; rather, I discuss it with her to gain her comments and feedback. After explaining my proposal, I often use the catchphrase, "What are your thoughts on this?" Gaining her input allows me to regroup if necessary to modify my original ideas and present a second verbal proposal that is "our" proposal rather than mine.

When I present a verbal proposal, I strive to build not only confidence but also excitement. Because I believe it is true, I want my prospect to feel that she really needs this offering, and I want her to understand that I am the best qualified to provide it. Here, I often end with the phrase, "How would you like to go forward on this?"

At this point, I love to hear the words, "Let's get started on . . . " or "Yes, let's do that and also. . . . "

But, of course, it's not always that simple. Often my prospect asks for a written proposal.

Present a Written Proposal

There are as many ways to write proposals as there are prospects on the street. I do have a simple, streamlined format that I use, but I always ask my prospects if they want to provide me with a template that they're used to. They're generally happy to do this and I think that giving them the information in a format they're familiar with—

one that's easy for them to use—can make a difference in the outcome.

While we won't go into the details of actually writing a proposal, I do want to mention that very seldom do I just "send" a proposal; I always prefer to present it in person. Over the years, I've tracked my success using both of these approaches, and there is a very high return on the time and effort it takes to go back and personally present a proposal. One of the important elements of presentation is that it gives me the opportunity to answer any questions or further objections that my prospect might have, right on the spot. And if there are one or two areas that she wants to negotiate, we can often discuss and settle them at that point, bringing us closer to the close.

NEGOTIATE WITH EASE

To run a great business, you have to be a solid negotiator. And although negotiation scares many women, it's really not that difficult. I've developed an approach that works for me and I believe can dramatically improve your negotiation skills and help you move your business forward.

Always begin negotiation with the end in mind. You've obtained a lot of information in your preliminary research and meeting with the prospect, so you're entering the negotiation phase with a good sense of your value to them. Prior to the negotiation, I always write out my best-case scenario for the outcome and list my negotiation points starting with the most important to me.

As you've done throughout the sales process, the best negotiation tactic is to ask questions and LISTEN to the answers. Listening allows you to identify what your counterpart really wants and needs. Never assume that her wants and needs are the same as yours. Ask the question and then really listen to the answer.

It's important to remember that everything is negotiable. A negotiation is often honed down to one issue—price. However, other negotiation items may be just as important or more to your counterpart. So don't just focus on price; develop other deal points such as delivery terms, hours of service, or payment terms.

And speaking of price, charge a fair price for your offering. Pricing is one of the biggest mistakes I see women make in negotiation; they undercut the value of their offerings. If you do make price concessions, studies show that uneven dollar amounts are challenged less frequently than even amounts. So rather than stating your price as $15,000, try providing an "uneven" figure, such as $14,582, and state that figure as your lowest price.

If you do make concessions, make them slowly. When you concede quickly and easily, your prospects will assume that they can push through even more concessions. Take your time on making concessions and always ask for something, no matter how small, in return. I have requested concessions ranging from an earlier start date ("Next month's calendar is actually light, so I could make that concession for you if we can start on November 1.") to payment terms ("I could make that concession if you agree to pay 50 percent up front and the balance net 15.").

Above all, be fair and honest. The goal in sales negotiation, as in all areas of business, is to generate win-win situations. To reach this goal, both you and your prospect must feel satisfied with the outcome.

CLOSE THE DEAL

As you move through the negotiation, always be aware of your prospect's immediate position. When you reach the point of agreement, stop and make a closing statement like, "Well, I'm excited about our agreement and can't wait to start."

This is the magic moment. The moment you've worked toward has finally occurred. Aside from the birth of my children, closing a big deal is the highest high I've ever experienced.

I'll always remember the exciting, exhilarating rush that came over me when I closed a huge deal with Digital Equipment that allowed me to open our Boston office. On the surface, I tried to remain calm, while inside I was jumping up and down. I walked from the building into the parking lot and sat in my rental car for probably half an hour, just basking in the joy. I sat there with a smile on my face, occasionally slapping the steering wheel saying, "This is great! This is *so* great!"

And beyond my own personal elation, I also recognized how wonderful this would be for my new client. And I was right. That initial sale was the start of a long, wonderful relationship.

■ **MENTOR:**	*Margery Kraus*
■ **BUSINESS:**	*APCO Worldwide*
■ **LOCATION:**	*Washington, D.C., U.S.A.*
■ **INDUSTRY:**	*Public Affairs and Communication*

ONE WOMAN WHO DID IT RIGHT

Just over 20 years ago, Margery Kraus left a job she loved at the Close Up Foundation because she had a vision for a new kind of consulting firm. The firm would be a place where clients could go with their biggest issues or opportunities. As someone once told Margery, ". . . where we would go when we absolutely could not afford to fail."

Today APCO Worldwide is one of the largest employee-owned communication firms in the world and is involved in some of the biggest issues of our times. APCO negotiates with or advocates for governments at all levels, supports market entry, and offers a full range of services that position, protect, and shape the reputation of their clients.

Margery has received numerous awards recognizing her achievements. She's been named International PR Professional of the Year by *PR Week,* a Top Woman Business Builder by *Fast Company,* and one of 50 Women Who Mean Business by *The Washington Business Journal.*

How did Margery Kraus, a woman of modest upbringing whose parents owned a small general store, become such an international powerhouse? Simply put, she took risks, had the will to accomplish her goals, and, most important, mastered the art of closing the deal.

HOW SHE DID IT

Margery always had a knack for sales, having worked in her father's store from as far back as she can remember. She learned about satisfying customers and "closing the sale," along with her school lessons. And her ability to close a deal has allowed her to build businesses for others and advance her own.

From the beginning, Margery learned that nothing is impossible. Her parents were born in Poland; her mother was raised in Cuba when she couldn't get into the United States. Margery was the first in her family to go to college and the first for whom there were no limits imposed by family, culture, or state. Her parents encouraged her, even when they didn't have a clue about her pursuits. She remembers her mother's constant mantra, "Where there is a will, there is a way."

Margery's first major job was for a nonprofit called the Close Up Foundation, a wonderful organization that seeks to involve young people in learning about government and politics. She worked at Close Up from its inception and helped build successful programs in all 50 states. Because the program had no reputation and few resources, Margery learned to do just about everything.

She found ways to raise money from senior corporate officials and developed a program involving Congress and more than 2,000 high schools. She learned the best way to succeed was to create win-win situations. Each deal was based upon finding that unique element that allowed people to say "Yes" to the proposition. She learned how much easier it is to make a deal when the other party thinks you're doing him or her a favor.

Margery left Close Up in 1984 to start APCO as an affiliate of a major law firm. She used what she'd learned at Close Up, coupled with her inner sense, to carve out a place for APCO. Business grew slowly in the first seven years. But, client by client, it made progress and started to build a reputation.

The success came from figuring out what would make people *buy* its service rather than try to *sell* it. Margery has always approached sales this way—by putting herself in the chair of her prospect. For example, she once bid on a communication contract for a baby food manufacturer. In the course of discussion, she learned that the company was struggling to enter a market in which APCO had special expertise. Rather than selling the client on her company's know-how, Margery arranged a session, led by one of her experts, that helped the manufacturer understand the market and the opportunities within it. During this session, she specifically shied away from "selling" her services; however, at the end, her firm was hired because she had demonstrated a specific expertise that the client wanted to buy.

The "closing" of each deal increased her confidence and she became convinced that solving other people's problems was a viable business. However, developing one business inside another was not going to work for the long term. In 1991, Grey Global Group, a publicly traded company, acquired a majority interest in APCO. Over the next 13 years, APCO grew from a $3 million business to more than $50 million. It opened 24 offices around the world, and learned how to consult with significant clients from business and government.

Then came the biggest challenge of Margery's career. She convinced Grey to allow her to put together a management buyout (MBO). But that was the easy part. Actually putting together the MBO was a complicated transaction that required taking on her employer, obtaining employee backing, raising private equity, fighting off unfriendly offers, and satisfying their majority shareholder. Margery had to use all the lessons in negotiation she had ever learned:

- Identify the "must-haves" for the other side.
- Know where you need to end up and what is important to you.
- Do not compromise on the essentials, but compromise like crazy on the things not central to the final deal.
- Know your own style and what works for you; don't try to replicate someone else's success.
- Create an environment that is friendly to the deal. (Get people close to the other party to validate the importance of the deal.)
- Convince yourself that where there is a will, there is a way.
- Don't be intimidated by the big boys.

In the final outcome, APCO won its freedom—despite the investment bankers, lawyers, and others who thought the deal was impossible. It was the ultimate deal of Margery's career and she has never experienced a sweeter moment than signing the stock certificates for APCO's new employee shareholders.

WHAT SHE ACHIEVED

Today, APCO is a $70 million business growing at 20 percent a year. One of the principles Margery refused to compromise during the buyout was providing employees with significant ownership in the business. As a result, nearly every member of senior management has shares of the business, and the number of employees with ownership will grow with the business.

Having control of the firm's destiny has enabled Margery's team to attract some of the best and brightest talent from around the world. Their 400-person consulting arsenal includes former high-ranking government officials, ambassadors, business leaders, and journalists.

Success seems to breed success. Seventy percent of APCO's business comes from referrals of happy clients. And the buyout created an even stronger entrepreneurial environment and "can-do" spirit throughout the firm. Most important, Margery and her team have achieved success without sacrificing their ethics and values.

In thinking back on the stages of the business, Margery realizes the gap between success and failure was not always wide. At several times during her career, and certainly in the history of the firm, it would have been much easier, and less frightening, not to push the envelope. However, her vision and drive to achieve what she wanted have always provided the staying power in tough times.

Margery makes it clear that, as a consulting firm, APCO's assets are its people. And the MBO was proof positive to her staff that she really means this. As for herself, she wakes up every day knowing that she is building something of value not just for herself, but for many people she respects and who have helped build the organization.

Over the next five years, Margery's team plans to double APCO's business. More important, they believe they can change the way consulting is conducted in the field of public relations and public affairs by creating a very high-end offering, specializing in communication and helping clients "win" in the global marketplace.

Margery recently received a lifetime achievement award from *PR News*. It was a time for quiet reflection. She thought of her mother's words of wisdom: "Where there is a will, there is a way." Margery truly believes that her success has come from knowing what she wants and having the will to make it happen, even when the odds are stacked the other way.

She grew up in a different time—a time when women were definitely not at the deal table. But she has learned to survive by her wits, her will, and a lot of hard work. Through experience, she's also learned that everyone has her own personal style, and successful women understand how to leverage their own style. Ultimately, closing the deal is an art that every woman should adapt to her own style. It might not be easy at first, but mastering it will make all the difference in your business and in your life.

Capitalizing on the Deal

20

When you consider the time and money you spend to acquire a customer, it makes good sense to invest at least as much effort taking care of them after the sale. It doesn't matter how many new customers you add to your business if your existing ones are walking out.

FOLLOW UP AFTER THE SALE

One of the most important things you can do for new customers is to help them feel they've made a good decision. You want them to trust that working with you will improve their businesses and their lives. The best way to gain this trust is to do what you said you'd do. And the second best is to give them more than they've paid for.

Whenever I close a deal, I like to come up with one more thing I can do for a client. Then I call and say, "I had this one extra idea, and would like to do this for you without charge." This approach really makes an imprint on the mind of a new client. Just think about it, when was the last time someone offered to give you something free *after* you signed the contract?

I also like to send a small gift, with a note, to her assistant(s). In the note, I mention a specific thing the assistant did for me—even if it was only to schedule the meeting—and thank her for her part in bringing our companies together. When was the last time someone did this for one of *your* assistants?

CHARM EXISTING CUSTOMERS

I'll bet your top customers are one of your most valuable business assets. I know mine are. So, at the beginning of every month, I sit down and make a list of the five clients that I can least afford to lose—the ones that would send me into a tailspin if they walked out. Then I decide on a specific action that I will take *that month* to enrich my relationship with each of those clients. I do this month in and month out.

My clients laughingly refer to me as a card freak. I'm always on the lookout for unique, quirky greeting cards and actually have a file drawer with cards categorized by occasion. Most of these are not "businesslike" but are just cards that I'd send to friends. And because my clients *are* my friends, this is what they receive from me.

I have a vendor who does the same thing with branded gifts. Joyce Shevelev-Putzer, owner of Famous Marks, knows that my favorite color is green. I wear green when I speak, write only with a green pen, and actually found a Web site that sells green paperclips. Joyce goes out of her way to feed my green addiction. Whether it's with green M&Ms, a green gym bag, or a package of green Post-it notes, whenever I receive a green gift from her, I always know that she's spent time and energy finding something just for me.

And this is the kind of thing we should all do for our customers—something that makes them feel like they're one in a million. Something fun, something that no one else will think of (or if they do think of it, they'll be too stuffy to follow through). Who said business has to be "businesslike"? I want clients to think of me as a good friend who considers them special—because they are.

GAIN REFERRALS

Although everyone agrees that referrals are the best way to identify prospects, many women neglect this important route. According to research, 86 percent of clients will give you a referral if you ask for one, but only 12 percent of them are ever asked. Are you one of those women who, out of embarrassment or fear of asking for a favor, would rather make dreaded cold calls than develop a strategy to increase referrals?

If so, let me show you some comfortable approaches that work for me.

Give Referrals to Get Them

Over the years, I've learned that the best way to get referrals is to give them. To do this, I send an e-mail to individuals I know telling them "I'd love to refer some customers to you. Can you tell me the characteristics of your perfect client?"

I almost always get a quick response that enables me to connect them by e-mail with a few individuals who are good prospects. Then, in a separate e-mail, I tell them to let me know how those connections work out and ". . . here's what my perfect client looks like, in case you come across anyone who fits this bill." They follow my lead and almost immediately send an e-mail or two introducing me to very good prospects.

Schedule a Referral Meeting with Your Clients

Women are sometimes surprised when I suggest that they sit down with individual clients for a referral meeting. But this works like a charm for me. In this meeting, I explain to my clients what my ideal customer looks like (industry, revenue, title, "executives who are dealing with such and such a problem . . . ") and the value that I bring to them ("I help these individuals . . . ").

If you feel uncomfortable using this approach, you can schedule a meeting with an agenda allowing you to learn what *their* ideal customer looks like and the value that they bring. Then for the second half of the meeting flip the agenda and ask them to think of prospects for you.

Once you develop an ongoing process to gain referrals, you'll never have to make another cold call for the rest of your life!

EXPAND YOUR PRODUCT LINE

I always encourage women to consider expanding their product lines, and I recently learned of one that is truly out of the box. A friend of mine, Sharon Avent, is president and CEO of Smead Manufacturing Company, a firm that manufactures and distributes office filing systems and supplies. With her latest product, Sharon and her team proved that even filing can be fun—they created a selection of scented folders. *The Fragrance Collection* was originally developed as a special promotion for Office Depot, and it was such a hit that Smead turned it into a seasonal collection. By identifying a new way to present an existing product, Sharon's team turned a mundane task into a pleasurable one. If she can develop a new twist to an age-old product like file folders, what opportunities are there for you in your business?

HONOR KEY CUSTOMERS

I've chosen to end this book with my most powerful marketing approach: honoring key customers. Over the years I've developed creative ways to honor my clients and my return on investment on these events has been the best money I've spent on my business.

Here are a few of my ideas.

Take Clients' Pictures

Let's fess up. Most women like to have their pictures taken, and women entrepreneurs are no exception. So whenever I attend an event, especially one honoring a client, I bring my camera. My goal is to get one good shot of my client, and a second good shot of my client *with me*. Then, at the least, I e-mail the picture to her; and sometimes, especially if it's a great shot of the two of us, I'll have it enlarged and framed and give it to her as a gift. There's nothing like seeing a picture of the two of you together when you visit a client's office.

But then I take my picture strategy one step further. I put pictures of my clients on all my marketing materials, in my Power-Point presentations, and on my Web site. To see how this works, check out the smiling faces on my home page, *http://www.Woman BusinessOwner.com.*

Conduct a Client Appreciation Day

Everybody likes to be appreciated and how better than to have your own day? I like to plan a client appreciation day after I've been working with a client for a few months.

I start by contacting one of her key employees and telling that individual what I'm planning. I then schedule a meeting with my client early on a particular morning. I arrive for that meeting with a cake, balloons, and flowers. Sometimes I have these delivered and sometimes I bring them. If I have a picture of myself with that client, I have it enlarged and framed and bring that along as well.

Then I ask my client to call her key staff into the room and I announce that this is "Johnson Plastics Appreciation Day." I then discuss all the reasons I appreciate my client and her staff, and I announce that in addition to the items I've brought, lunch will be delivered for the staff at noon. On occasion, I've also brought in a massage therapist to provide chair massages for all the staff.

My clients say what they like best about this acknowledgment is that I'm not only showing my appreciation for them, but I'm also allowing them to share that appreciation with their staff.

Submit Clients for Awards

There's an award for everything. And how better to strengthen a relationship than by submitting your clients for awards? I do this on a regular basis and have developed a simple process that takes little more than a phone call or an e-mail.

First, of course, I identify an appropriate award. This might be an industry award or it might be a regional award—something like the Top 25 Women in Business. Just about every region has this type of award, generally presented by a publication such as a business journal. In our city, we also have one called Women Extraordinaire, which is awarded to the top ten women each year. Just think about the loyalty you would feel to a vendor who nominated you as a Woman Extraordinaire!

Then (and here comes the easy part) I tell my client that I want to nominate her, but I'd like to have her PR firm or someone on her staff complete the nomination so she's presented in the best light. Of course, she is always happy to do this and it saves me the time of writing the nomination. Then when I receive the information, I simply submit the application.

But what if she doesn't win? Does that make me look bad? Over the years, my batting average has been well over 90 percent, and in the few instances when my client hasn't won, I tell her I'll submit her again next year. But because I didn't write up the actual nomination, she doesn't harbor bad feelings against me and I don't feel "guilty" that she didn't win.

And, win or lose, I always gain tremendous loyalty.

DOUBLE YOUR REVENUE

Every Woman Dreams of Moving Her Business to the Next Level. Here's **Your** *Chance to Do Just That!*

The Woman's Advantage Contest

Looking for the perfect contest to grow your business and get your name out there? *The Woman's Advantage* has joined with key corporate partners to create a contest that can propel your business, or that of a client, to the next level. To be eligible, you or you and your female partners must be majority owners of a business as of May 1, 2006.

To enter, simply tell us how you have applied one concept from this book to improve your business. As the winner, you, or your client, will receive two valuable awards:

- The opportunity to be mentored by Mary Cantando for 12 months with the goal of doubling your revenue in one year
- Prizes from major corporate sponsors

To learn more about the contest and nominate either yourself or a client, visit our Web site: *http://www.WomansAdvantage.biz.*

Introduce Key Clients to Influentials

I'm always on the lookout for ways that I can bring influential women together. About a year ago, I met the vice president of a large public company, a woman who had recently relocated to our area. Because I knew that Alicia would value connections to local executive women, I invited three of my local clients, all women who own sizable businesses, to a special dinner to honor her. I hosted this dinner at the downtown executive club and personally called each woman to invite her.

The results were more than I had hoped for. After meeting Alicia at my dinner, all of the women scheduled individual follow-up lunches with her. One gained a contract following my welcoming dinner and another gained several contracts over the course of the following year. And, equally important, they all became fast friends. This event was certainly a win-win-win, for Alicia, for all the clients I invited, and, of course, for me.

I remember the comment one client made as we shared an elevator on the way out, "You really hit a home run tonight."

BE CREATIVE

I encourage you to implement the ideas discussed here. But beyond these suggestions, I hope you're inspired to develop other interesting approaches to capitalize on *your* deals. Creative efforts like this will help you grow your business . . . and have fun doing it!

■ **MENTOR:**	*Dato' Dr. Jannie Tay*
■ **BUSINESS:**	*The Hour Glass Limited*
■ **LOCATION:**	*Singapore City, Singapore*
■ **INDUSTRY:**	*Luxury Retailer*

ONE WOMAN WHO DID IT RIGHT

Born in Malaysia, educated in Australia, and a citizen of Singapore, Dato' Dr. Jannie Tay is a true international entrepreneur. A businesswoman whose achievements are recognized around the world, Jannie, along with her husband, Henry Tay, built a one-shop retail operation into a leading international retailer of high-quality timepieces, writing instruments, and jewelry.

The Hour Glass, an award-winning luxury retail empire she started in 1979, is a chain of boutiques across Singapore, Australia, Hong Kong, Japan, Malaysia, Thailand, Bangkok, and Kuala Lumpur. And, if that weren't enough, The Hour Glass is one of *four* major business endeavors that Jannie directs. After building her luxury retail operation, she capitalized on her international reputation to build other businesses based on her personal passions.

Jannie's love for Australia and commitment to the environment led her to start her second business in 1995. For the past decade, she has been developing Oyster Cove, a 400-acre luxury eco-resort on the Gold Coast of Australia. Here she combines waterfront living with plans for retail shopping and a spa. She also envisions a 26-hectare sanctuary providing for kangaroos, koala bears, and other Australian wildlife. Jannie foresees Oyster Cove as a "Golden Age" estate development providing every facility imaginable for a luxurious life in an eco-friendly setting.

After initiating Oyster Cove, Jannie decided to combine her background in pharmacology, her understanding of traditional medicine, and her business expertise with her passion for well-being. These interests drove her to establish Hypha Holdings, a company that focuses on natural living and biomedical products. Chief among Hypha's offerings is her Scientific Tradition brand of traditional medicinals based on her concept of Global Integrated Medicine.

Then, in 2004, Jannie launched Save the Planet Investments. Through this effort, she pursues the goal of environment wellness. With a plan to supergrow cultivars of teak and eucalyptus, her organization seeks to slow global warming. To date, she's planted one million trees, with a goal of two million for next year. And there is no doubt that Jannie will achieve her ultimate vision of planting ten million trees each year.

As if the relentless demands of running four highly successful businesses weren't enough, Jannie leads a highly faceted life as a wife, mother, grandmother, author, socialite, and patron of the underprivileged. Everything she approaches is based on her spiritual nature and her ability to build on what she has already achieved. Jannie understands how to capitalize on opportunities she has created.

HOW SHE DID IT

One of the most successful and well-known women in all of Asia, Jannie Tay was raised in a strict but nurturing Malaysian family during an era of gender discrimination. Because of strong, encouraging parents, Jannie was able to overcome the norms of her society and pursue a college degree. After earning her bachelor's degree in Physiology and her master's in Pharmacology from Monash University in Melbourne, Australia, she moved to Singapore with her husband, Henry, a newly graduated doctor whose family owned a watch business.

At this point in her life, Jannie didn't envision herself as a businesswoman, let alone an entrepreneur. Her only goal was to be a good wife and mother. But because her husband sought to develop his medical practice, Jannie took his place in the family watch business. So, with no previous retail experience, she found herself as a watch "salesgirl."

As she worked in the family store, Jannie began to consider possibilities for a business of her own. She envisioned a chain of exclusive watch boutiques, and she developed a clear vision of how her business would differ from the competition. She imagined a luxury operation with deluxe settings, exquisite products, and a prestigious reputation. Jannie knew she couldn't achieve her dream on her own, but in partnering with Henry, whose left brain perfectly complemented her right brain, she knew she could achieve all this and more. Henry saw the opportunity and made the decision to leave his medical practice to join Jannie as they launched The Hour Glass.

As she built her business, Jannie kept a sharp eye on her clientele as they became more sophisticated and garnered higher incomes. By continuing to work directly with clients, she was able to anticipate their evolving wants. As a result, she made the decision to discard the standard glass cases, concrete floors, and ceiling fans that were predominant in the industry, replacing them with upscale carpet and elegant displays. By paying attention to their affluent clients, including the royalty and Asian superrich, The Hour Glass moved directly in step with them, and the company's resulting revenue reflected this.

And so, this "salesgirl" with a vision worked side by side with her husband to build a retail empire that expanded across the Asia Pacific. In doing so, she created the legacy of The Hour Glass.

WHAT SHE ACHIEVED

Jannie Tay believes, "As captains of our destiny, it is the responsibility of women to take charge of our own lives, to chart the course we would like to pursue and then to steer ourselves toward achieving our goals. We may not have the best start in life, but opportunities knock and we need to recognize them and act on them with integrity and honesty."

Jannie's life has been all about recognizing and capitalizing on opportunities. She took a single retail outlet and expanded it across the Pacific to create an international retail dynasty, now a public company trading on the Singapore Exchange. She then capitalized on her reputation to build additional businesses in three very different realms. But through it all, the constant has been her spirituality and her passion, two elements that call her to give back to the community and the planet.

Mindful of the challenges women face in balancing their businesses, families, and personal lives, Jannie has made a significant commitment to nurturing women in business. As an indication of her commitment, she founded both the International Women's Forum, in Singapore, whose members cross national boundaries to share ideas and knowledge, and the Women's Business Connection, which strives to develop and nurture aspiring woman managers and executives. And she was selected as a member of the Women's Leadership Initiative at Harvard University's John Kennedy School of Government.

Because she understands the critical value of globalization, Jannie cofounded the East-West Foundation, which serves as a link between Asian businesspeople and business partners in Australia. In addition, she initiated the Globalisation Learning Journey, a secondary school program preparing students to function on a global basis.

As the first and only woman Executive Board Member of the Commonwealth Business Council, Jannie has worked to involve the private sector in the promotion of international trade and investment. As a result, she was appointed as the first Chair of the Commonwealth Business Women Leaders Network, and the first woman president of both the Asean Business Forum and the Singapore Retailers Association.

Jannie was named one of the 50 Leading Women Entrepreneurs of the World and one of the 25 Most Powerful Women in the World. But one of her greatest honors occurred in 2003, when she was conferred the title of Dato', Darjah Sultan Ahmad Shah Pahang Peringkat Kedua (DSAP) (Knight Commander of the Most Honourable Order of Sultan Ahmad Shah) by His Royal Highness, Sultan of Pahang.

As if all this personal recognition were not enough, Jannie's efforts have also generated plaudits for her business. Under her leadership, The Hour Glass received the inaugural Singapore Brand Award, signifying that it had one of the highest brand values in the country. And The Hour Glass was the first watch retailer in the world to receive ISO 9002 certification, and the first to receive the People Developer certification. The Hour Glass was also singled out as the Singapore Specialty Store of the Year and has won numerous popular vote awards from organizations such as Diners Club and American Express.

Today, with 14 locations spanning the Asia Pacific, The Hour Glass has become the ultimate "family business." The next generation of Jannie and Henry's family, their daughter, Audrey, and son, Michael, has become involved. Since incorporating the novel ideas of her two adult children, the stores have advanced even further and new boutiques have opened in Bangkok and Kuala Lumpur. And Sabrina, her youngest daughter, gives her time toward volunteer work in Canossian School, where she provides programs for hearing-impaired children.

But beyond the business growth, personal recognition, and industry awards, Jannie is proof positive that women entrepreneurs can have it all—successful businesses, joyful marriages, and happy children. A true entrepreneur with sharp business acumen and an optimist who believes that anything is achievable, Jannie makes a difference by capitalizing on every aspect of life.

Glossary of Terms for Entrepreneurial Women

alliances A formal or informal agreement to work together to provide a joint deliverable or service

bundling The clustering of previously separate projects or contracts into a single entity for contracting efficiency

C200 The Committee of 200; international organization of women who run businesses of at least $15 million in annual revenue

consolidation of suppliers Initiatives to reduce the number of suppliers with a goal of lowering overall costs

core competency The primary capability of an organization

eWomenNetwork Organization of women who meet for "Accelerated Networking Events" in major cities across the United States

NAWBO National Association of Women Business Owners; national organization for women who own their own businesses, with chapters in most U.S. cities

NMSDC National Minority Supplier Development Council; third-party certifying organization for minority-owned businesses

reverse auction A bidding opportunity in which a customer presents a need to vendors; vendors then bid, typically online, providing the best price they can offer. Generally, the lowest bidder is awarded the contract.

second-tier supplier Second-level contractor; subcontractor; also referred to as Tier 2 supplier

site visit Meeting between a WBENC affiliate volunteer and a WBE to verify WBENC application items

spend The amount that a corporation or government entity purchases from a WBE; this amount is typically tracked both by individual vendor and in aggregate.

strategic sourcing A systematic approach to minimize costs, streamline processes, and improve quality; results in the clustering of like purchases from fewer vendors

supplier diversity The current industry trend to purchase from suppliers of diverse backgrounds. Depending on the organization, these may include women, racial minorities, disabled veterans, and small, disadvantaged businesses.

Tier 1 Direct supplier to a customer; contractor

Tier 2 Second-level supplier; subcontractor; also referred to as second-tier supplier

WEBUY WBENC online resource providing listings of opportunities for WBEs

WBE Women's Business Enterprise; certification industry terminology for a business that is majority-owned (51 percent or more) and managed by a woman or women

WBENC Women's Business Enterprise National Council; the primary third-party certifying organization for women-owned businesses

WBENC-Discuss Online resource providing information about WBENC programs and events

WPO Women Presidents' Organization; organization of women who own and run multimillion-dollar businesses, with chapters in most major U.S. and Canadian cities

Zenith Group A group of high-revenue WPO peers with WBENC certification who meet twice a year to drive business breakthroughs

Resource Guide

ORGANIZATIONS AND PUBLICATIONS FOR WOMEN ENTREPRENEURS

- Center for Women's Business Research, *http://www.womensbusinessresearch.org*
- Committee of 200, *http://www.C200.org*
- Enterprising Women, *http://www.enterprisingwomen.com*
- eWomenNetwork, *http://www.ewomennetwork.com*
- Latina Style, *http://www.latinastyle.com*
- National Association of Female Executives, *http://www.nafe.org*
- National Association of Women Business Owners, *http://www.nawbo.org*
- National Association of Women in Construction, *http://www.nawic.org*
- National Women's Business Council, *http://www.nwbc.gov*
- Online Women's Business Center, *http://www.onlinewbc.gov*
- Springboard Enterprises, *http://www.springboardenterprises.org*
- Women Construction Owners & Executives, *http://www.wcoeusa.org*
- Women Entrepreneurs, Inc., *http://www.we-inc.org*
- Women Impacting Public Policy, *http://www.wipp.org*
- Women in Franchising, *http://www.womeninfranchising.com*
- Women in Technology International, *http://www.witi.com*

- Women Presidents' Organization,
  http://www.womenpresidentsorg.com
- Women's Business Enterprise National Council,
  http://www.wbenc.org
- Women's Entrepreneurship in the 21st Century,
  http://www.women-21.gov
- Women's Leadership Exchange,
  http://www.womensleadershipexchange.com
- World Association of Women Entrepreneurs,
  http://www.fcem.org

GOVERNMENT CLASSIFICATIONS

8(a)

To qualify, your business must be owned and controlled by socially and economically disadvantaged U.S. citizens. This program helps such businesses access federal contracts.

Disadvantaged Business Enterprise (DBE)

To qualify, your business must be small (as determined by your SIC code) and disadvantaged. Members of a minority are considered socially disadvantaged; however, women are not unless they can prove a pattern of social discrimination.

Historically Underutilized Business (HUB)

This certification is valuable in bidding on state government contracts; however, the application requires a lot of time and detailed reporting of financial records.

Historically Underutilized Business Zone (HUBZone)

To qualify, you must have a principal office in a HUBZone and 35 percent of employees of that office must reside in a HUBZone. The goal of HUBZones is to create jobs in specific areas by providing federal contracting preferences to businesses in those areas.

Small Disadvantaged Business (SBD)

To qualify, you must be certified by the Small Business Administration and have a net worth of under $750,000.

GOVERNMENT DATABASES

Central Contractor Registration (CCR)

CCR is required for contracts with the Department of Defense, Department of Transportation, or NASA. Other federal agencies accept the CCR, but have not made it mandatory.

Fedbizopps.com

This Web site allows you to receive e-mail procurement notices. You determine which agencies you want to receive postings from. If you decide to receive all notices, you will receive hundreds of e-mail messages a month.

PRO-Net

PRO-Net is the contractor registry for small businesses. Registering in PRO-Net provides access to every federal government contracting officer. The online application is easy to understand and takes just a few minutes to complete.

Others

Some federal departments and agencies have their own contractor databases. You should contact each department or agency you want to work with to determine if it has a separate contractor registry database.

CHECKLIST FOR CERTIFICATION DOCUMENTS

General Information

- ☐ History of business
- ☐ Professional and business licenses
- ☐ Résumés of owners, directors, and key executives
- ☐ Copy of bank signature authorization card
- ☐ Current union agreements, if applicable

Owner Eligibility

- ☐ Evidence of gender for woman (women) owners (for example, birth certificate)
- ☐ Evidence of U.S. citizenship (for example, passport) or Legal Resident Alien status (legal resident alien card)

Financial Structuring

- ☐ P&L and balance sheet for last complete year of operation
- ☐ Copies of the following documents that have been active within the past three years:
  - Debt instruments
  - Equipment rental and purchase agreements
  - Real estate leases
- ☐ Three years of income tax returns for the business (if less than three years old, substitute personal federal income tax returns for the other years)

Management Information

- ☐ Copies of all management/consulting agreements and service agreements that have been active within the past three years
- ☐ Copies of any affiliate/subsidiary agreements

Personnel

☐ List of all full-time and part-time employees by name, position, and length of service
☐ Itemized employee payroll for month prior to application submission
☐ W-2s and/or 1099s for every officer, director, or owner who received compensation from the company for the most recent year

LEGAL STRUCTURE

For Sole Proprietor

☐ Assumed name documents

For Partnership

☐ Partnership agreements
☐ Limited partnership certificate, if applicable
☐ Buyout rights agreement
☐ Profit-sharing agreement
☐ Proof of capital investment by all parties

For LLC

☐ Articles of organization
☐ Certificate of organization, if required by your state
☐ LLC regulations or operating agreement or member agreement
☐ Member list with titles
☐ Proof of equity investment by women owners
☐ If out-of-state LLC, proof of authority to do business in the state where the application is made
☐ Schedule of advances made to LLC by members in preceding three years

For Corporation

☐ Certificate of incorporation

☐ Articles of incorporation

☐ Minutes from shareholders organization meeting

☐ Minutes from first board of directors meeting

☐ Minutes from shareholders or board of directors meeting establishing current ownership

☐ Minutes from the most recent meeting of shareholders

☐ Minutes from most recent meeting of board of directors

☐ Corporation bylaws

☐ Certificate from secretary to certify the names of all current board members

☐ Both sides of *ALL* stock certificates

☐ Stock transfer ledger, if applicable

☐ Proof of stock purchase or equity investment for women owners

☐ Voting agreements, stock options, warrants, buy-sell agreements, and right of first refusal

☐ If out-of-state corporation, proof of authority to do business in the state where the application is made

☐ Schedule of advances made to corporation by shareholders for the preceding three years

Index

About the Author

As a featured speaker, author, columnist, and consultant, Mary Cantando engages audiences throughout the country with her insight and understanding regarding the power and potential of women business owners.

An entrepreneurial executive since 1989, Mary is a recognized authority on women's business initiatives. Having personally closed sales of up to $50 million, Mary is a respected sales and marketing expert who has helped countless women entrepreneurs develop new, successful revenue streams for their enterprises.

Mary is a member of the National Speakers Association and presents at regional, national, and international events for women business owners. She delivers powerful, cutting-edge information that provides immediate results for her audiences. Mary is on the International Board of the Women Presidents' Organization, sits on the Advisory Board of *Enterprising Women* magazine, and serves on the National Forum of the Women's Business Enterprise National Council. And she is frequently tapped as a resource by media outlets such as the *Wall Street Journal, Entrepreneur* magazine, and *Fast Company.*

As a result of speaking with women business owners around the world, Mary Cantando has discovered one common denominator: They all have big dreams for their chosen enterprises. However, most also share another characteristic: They haven't been able to build their "nice little businesses" into multimillion-dollar ventures. Mary shows her audiences the secrets and strategies to do just that.

As a speaker, Mary realizes that every woman entrepreneur faces a unique set of business challenges. As a result, she presents

The Woman's Advantage keynotes and workshops by responding to the audience's requests on the fly. Participants request anecdotes they want to hear from a "clothesline" of icons, each representing a story from the book. Mary then tells that story and explains that lesson; thus, the audience-chosen icon directs the content of the presentation.

Each presentation of *The Woman's Advantage* is unique, powerful, and life-changing. But, most importantly, each is driven entirely by the topic and story selections of the audience. Mary's "anti-PowerPoint" approach encourages lively, thought-provoking conversation and literally has audience members on their feet! At the end, each woman understands the advantages she brings to the table and how to use these advantages to propel her business to multimillion-dollar status.

Mary has captivated and inspired audiences at the following:

- Women Presidents' Organization
- Women Business Owners Network
- NAWBO
- Executive Women International
- Women Trading Globally
- Michigan Women's Business Council
- Royal Bank of Canada
- Merrill Lynch
- Wachovia Bank
- Progress Energy
- Pan-Pacific Conference
- Many, many more

To schedule Mary's presentation of The Woman's Advantage, contact Info@WomanBusinessOwner.com.

DOUBLE YOUR REVENUE

EVERY WOMAN DREAMS OF MOVING HER BUSINESS TO THE NEXT LEVEL. HERE'S YOUR CHANCE TO DO JUST THAT!

The Woman Business Owner of the Year Contest brings to life the very themes and goals of *The Woman's Advantage* by connecting women business owners with major corporations eager to do business with them.

HERE'S HOW IT WORKS.

After reading this book, choose one new business concept that you learned and launch this new concept in your business. Then, go to **www.WomansAdvantage.biz**, and tell us how it benefited your business. Winners will be chosen based on how each applied the concept to her business and the impact it made to her business, which can be measured in revenue, profitability, new customers, employee retention, or a similar quantifiable measurement.

To be eligible, you, or you and your female partners, must be majority owners (51% or more) of a business as of May 1, 2006.

The grand prize winner will receive **one year of consulting with Mary Cantando**, the author of *The Woman's Advantage*, plus other prizes from major corporate sponsors. Mary will work one-on-one with the grand prize winner to help her capitalize on WBENC certification and WPO affiliation to **DOUBLE HER REVENUE** within 12 months.

For complete contest rules and to submit your entry, please visit www.WomansAdvantage.biz.

Entries must be submitted by November 1, 2006. Winners will be chosen by December 1, 2006, and will be recognized in conjunction with the WPO Annual Conference in April 2007.

The Women Presidents' Organization (WPO) is a nonprofit organization whose members are a diverse group of entrepreneurial women presidents. For more information, visit http://www.womenpresidentsorg.com.